Daily Mind Builders™
Social Studies

Daily Mind Builders™ Series
📖 Language Arts 📖 Science 📖 Social Studies

Written by
Jennifer Gottstein

Graphic Design by
Annette Langenstein

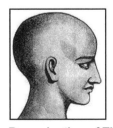

© 2009
THE CRITICAL THINKING CO.™
www.CriticalThinking.com
Phone: 800-458-4849 • Fax: 831-393-3277
P.O. Box 1610 • Seaside • CA 93955-1610
ISBN 978-1-60144-203-1

ABOUT THE AUTHOR

Jennifer Gottstein

Earlier in this century, when I began my teaching career, I went looking for that perfect activity that would start each school day off right. I had always loved activities that challenge the mind and thought these types of activities would be a good way to begin each school day. I soon discovered that higher level thinking activities are not as readily available as I had imagined. I then decided to find realistic situations that could be presented as a critical thinking activity. My first efforts in this direction were greeted by such enthusiasm that I soon realized I was onto something. My classes were asking for a new, realistic activity each day and were disappointed on the days when I failed to produce one.

From these early efforts, the three-book series of *Daily Mind Builders™* was born. I would like to thank the students for their continuous enthusiasm, cooperation, and support in the writing of these three volumes. I also want to acknowledge the support given to me by my parents and friends for this project. They acted as unpaid, yet cheerful research assistants, who helped me assemble much of the raw material that went into these books. I am very grateful for their guidance and support.

TABLE OF CONTENTS

The Value of These Activities

Each daily activity page includes two exercises. The first is a short story that requires careful reading and inferential reasoning to answer the question at the end. The second activity involves deductive thinking, and is designed to build vocabulary and stimulate associative thinking skills.

In addition to waking up sleepy brains for the day's lessons, these short, fun, daily activity pages develop the most important reading comprehension skill found on all standardized reading tests–synthesizing disparate information and using the result to produce a reasonable conclusion. Every *Daily Mind Builders™* exercise develops this key reading skill.

When to Use These Activities

Each *Daily Mind Builders™* is meant to be a short 5-10 minute activity, and can be a great way to start a lesson. However, there is no bad time to teach critical thinking and the *Daily Mind Builders™* can be inserted whenever time permits at any time during the school day, e.g.:

1. Motivational beginning activity used as an addition to the curriculum.
2. Culminating activity after a lesson or at the end of the day.
3. Fill-in activity when there is an awkward time break during the school day.
4. A valid educational activity for students who finish assigned activities earlier than their classmates.

The best use of this book is when presented as a non-threatening, non-graded, fun activity where students are praised for all logical answers even if they don't happen to be the correct answers. In critical thinking, the journey is as important as the destination, and all reasonable efforts at critical thinking should be commended.

Teaching Suggestions

Most of the stories in the first activity are based on historical events, with a few exceptions (myths/legends). The answer in the back of the book is the ideal conclusion one would expect to reach. Sentence evidence answers are based on this conclusion.

Optional Thinking Map

Some students benefit by filling out the optional *Daily Mind Builders™* Thinking Map (vi). On page vii is an example of a completed thinking map.

What is Critical Thinking?

Critical thinking is the identification and evaluation of evidence to guide decision making. A critical thinker uses broad, in-depth analysis of evidence to make decisions and to communicate his/her beliefs clearly and accurately.

It's All About Evidence

As a critical thinker, you need to identify and evaluate evidence to make and support your conclusions. Evidence can also prove your conclusion is correct. To help you understand what evidence is, read the six sentences below and try to find the evidence that tells you...

Who Helped Themselves to Peanut Butter and Jam?

[1]Eddie's mom looked at Eddie and his baby sister, Sarah. [2]There were crumbs on the floor, and Sarah had peanut butter and jam on her chin. [3]"Did you two help yourselves to the peanut butter and jam without asking?" asked Eddie's mom. [4]Eddie pointed to Sarah and said, "I didn't but Sarah did." [5]He quickly grabbed a clean paper towel and handed it to his mother so she could wipe Sarah's chin. [6]As he handed the towel to his mother, she saw peanut butter and jam on Eddie's fingers.

Information in sentence 2 tells us that that "Sarah had peanut butter and jam on her chin." We know from this evidence that she was into the peanut butter and jam. Sentence 6 tells us that Eddie had peanut butter and jam on his fingers. We know from this evidence that Eddie could be lying to his mother. The evidence in sentences 2 and 6 supports the conclusion that both Eddie and Sarah were into the peanut butter and jam.

The first activity on each page asks you to identify the best evidence for your conclusion. To help you identify a particular sentence, all of the sentences in the story are numbered. When looking for the best evidence for your conclusion, be sure to reread the story carefully.

Daily Mind Builders™ Thinking Map (Optional)

Question: _____

_____

⬇

Who?	
Did What?	
Where?	
When?	
Why?	

⬇

Conclusion:	

⬇

Evidence for Conclusion:	

Daily Mind Builders™ **Thinking Map Example**

Question: Can you infer what these wars are called? _____

_____

Who?	Two branches of the royal family of England
Did What?	Fought a series of wars
Where?	England
When?	Late 1400s
Why?	To settle the dispute over which royal house would provide the next ruler of England

Conclusion:	The Wars of the Roses

Evidence for Conclusion:

The House of York's emblem was a white rose and the House of Lancaster's was a red rose.

YOU HAVE TO CALL IT SOMETHING

*Read the true story below, then make an inference
based on the evidence in the story.*

[1]In the late 1400s, two branches of the royal family of England fought a series of wars over which one of them would provide the next ruler of England. [2]The dispute became violent as each royal house raised an army and went to war against each other. [3]The House of York took as its emblem a white rose, while the House of Lancaster took as its emblem a red rose. [4]Thus, soldiers fought under the banner of either a white rose or a red rose. [5]The wars finally ended when King Henry VII of Lancaster married a woman from the House of York and founded the Tudor Dynasty. [6]The wars between these two royal houses were given a sensible and easy to remember name. Can you infer what these wars are called?

Your conclusion: _____

Which sentences have the best evidence to support your conclusion? _____ _____

MIXED-UP CAPITALS

*Rearrange the letters below to correctly spell a capital city and its country.
Below each line are clues to the identity of the country.*

1. s a e i F P r r a c n   _____, _____

    City of Light, Eiffel Tower, fashion center, Notre Dame Cathedral, Louvre Museum

2. a o o n n n n L E g l d d   _____, _____

    Big Ben, Thames River, House of Parliament, Buckingham Palace, Queen Elizabeth

3. u i a o o s s s c w R M   _____, _____

    The Kremlin, Red Square, Lenin's Tomb, vodka, old name was Soviet Union

4. a o e y l t m l R   _____, _____

    spaghetti, pizza, Vatican City, an ancient world empire, the Colosseum

5. e a e i B G r r l n n y m   _____, _____

    sauerkraut, Oktoberfest, Mercedes-Benz, Rhine River, used to be East and West

THAT SCULPTURE REALLY MOVES ME

Read the true story below, then make an inference
based on the evidence in the story.

[1]Ancient sculptors from Babylon and Assyria carved many statues of animals such as bulls or lions. [2]They developed a unique technique that has not been seen for centuries. [3]When viewed from the front, these ancient statues of four-legged animals seem to be standing still as, of course, they are. [4]However, when viewed from the side, these animal statues appear to be moving. Can you figure out what these ancient sculptors added to their statues of bulls and lions to make it appear as if the animals were moving?

Your conclusion: _____

Which sentences have the best evidence to support your conclusion? _____ _____

ALL ACROSS

The letters in the word AMERICAN below are the first letters of words that
match the clues provided. Write the missing letters in the space provided.

A _____   largest state in the USA in land area

M _____   southern neighbor of the USA

E _____   historic canal in New York

R _____   Puerto's last name

I _____   corny state

C _____   northern neighbor of the USA

A _____   the capital of Georgia

N _____   largest city in the United States

NAME THAT CITY

Read the true story below, then make an inference
based on the evidence in the story.

[1]Many place names in North America began as Native American words for places European settlers decided to occupy. [2]The capital city of the province of Manitoba and one of the largest cities in Canada took its name from the Cree Indian words for "muddy water." [3]These words are *win nipee*. [4]The Europeans who settled in this area of muddy water decided to combine these two words, add a letter or two, and name their settlement pretty much according to the Cree Indian description of the location. Can you name this large Canadian city?

Your conclusion: _____

Which sentences have the best evidence to support your conclusion? _____ _____

PRESIDENTIAL NAME GAME

George Washington was the first president of the United States and his wife, Martha, was the first, "First Lady."

Using the letters in the names of the first president and his wife, write smaller words that match the clues on the lines below. The letters will always be in order either from left to right or right to left, and may be separated by other letters.

GEORGE & MARTHA WASHINGTON

1. _____   clean with soap and water

2. _____   a brief written message

3. _____   a wood-cutting tool

4. _____   a precious stone

5. _____   wheat, barley, oats, and others

6. _____   part of leg below the knee

7. _____   something done to potatoes or bugs

8. _____   a bird needs this to fly

9. _____   a male sheep, storage on a computer

10. _____   a too-hasty skin irritation

CAN YOU DIG IT?

Read the true story below, then make an inference
based on the evidence in the story.

[1]Wisconsin is justly famous for its dairy products. [2]However, Wisconsin is also known as the "Badger State," despite the fact that it doesn't have as many badgers or badger burrows as several other states. [3]Wisconsin citizens got the nickname "Badgers" back in the 1820s, when so many early workers in Wisconsin engaged in a particular activity and used their skills to house themselves in a rather unusual fashion. Can you infer what these early Wisconsin settlers were doing that earned them the name "Badgers?"

Your conclusion: _____

Which sentence has the best evidence to support your conclusion? _____

GEOGRAPHY RHYME TIME

plot	Egypt	Rome	miss	French	smirk	poem
Turk	thrill	peek	Pole	drain	Brazil	crypt
Greek	Swiss	mole	trench	Spain	Scot	

Write two rhyming words from the choice box that match the clues on each line. The first word in each set of clues has a geographic connection to the first answer word.

1. Italian rhyme _____   _____

2. Istanbul smile _____   _____

3. Madrid plumbing _____   _____

4. Cairo tomb _____   _____

5. Athens look _____   _____

6. Paris ditch _____   _____

7. Warsaw rodent _____   _____

8. Edinburgh plan _____   _____

9. Rio de Janeiro excitement _____   _____

10. Geneva gal _____   _____

ONE HOT ARCHITECT

*Read the true story below, then make an inference
based on the evidence in the story.*

[1]Sir Christopher Wren was an English architect, scientist, and mathematician who wasn't particularly busy until the year 1667, when demands for his talents suddenly became white hot. [2]Beginning in 1667, Sir Christopher Wren designed or re-designed an astounding 55 churches as well as many other important buildings in the city of London, England. [3]Many of the buildings Wren designed are still visited by tourists to London today. Can you think of something that happened in 1666 that caused Sir Christopher to become so busy for the rest of his life?

Your conclusion: _____

Which sentences have the best evidence to support your conclusion? _____ _____

SPEAKING BENGALI

cup	mail	cut	baby food	Europe
dress	hospital	airplane	depart	guide

The Bengali language, which is spoken by an estimated 220 million people, is the fourth most commonly spoken language in the world. It is the official language of the country of Bangladesh.

Write the English words from the choice box that best match the Bengali words below. Some Bengali words are spelled incorrectly to make them easier to pronounce.

1. Eeorohp   _____

2. jama   _____

3. gomohn   _____

4. kap   _____

5. plen   _____

6. bebifud   _____

7. kata   _____

8. gaid   _____

9. hashpatal   _____

10. pohst   _____

STOP, LOOK, AND LISTEN

*Read the true story below, then make an inference
based on the evidence in the story.*

[1]There are still many samples of Native American rock drawings to be found in North America. [2]Such drawings often told a story, conveyed messages, or were simply decorative. [3]One interesting rock drawing was found at the bottom of a steep trail in New Mexico. [4]The design of this drawing shows a goat walking upright and a horse and rider walking upside down. Can you infer what message this Native American rock writer was giving?

Your conclusion: _____

Which sentence has the best evidence to support your conclusion? _____

WHAT'S THE RELATIONSHIP?

The words in the shaded box have a logical connection to each other. Circle the word below the shaded box that shares the relationship. Then explain the relationship between the words.

1. Each is within reach.

Denmark	England	Germany	Kenya

Nepal   Ireland   Yemen

Why? _____

2. I said, you said.

Australia	India	Albania	Indonesia

Cambodia   Argentina   Latvia

Why? _____

3. All is well that ends well.

Egypt	Togo	Oman	Niger

Senagal   Kuwait   Russia

Why? _____

A WHATCHAMACALLIT?

*Read the true story below, then make an inference
based on the evidence in the story.*

[1]In 1893, Whitcomb Judson patented an invention that was a sort of slide fastener but he didn't really know what to call his invention. [2]In 1913, Gideon Sundback patented an improved version of Judson's invention but he didn't know what to call it either. [3]Finally, in 1922, the B.F. Goodrich Company used this still unnamed slide fastener on its rubber boots and gave it a name at last. Can you infer the name of this still-popular invention?

Your conclusion: _____

Which sentences have the best evidence to support your conclusion? _____ _____

PRESIDENTIAL NAME GAME

Using the letters in the names of our second president and his wife, write smaller words that match the definitions. The letters will always be in order either from left to right or right to left, and may be separated by other letters.

JOHN & ABIGAIL ADAMS

1. _____ unhappy

2. _____ cut of meat from a pig

3. _____ fastener that is hammered

4. _____ large

5. _____ frozen rain

6. _____ angry or crazy

7. _____ fruit preserves or trouble

8. _____ post bond or empty your boat

9. _____ reason for a paycheck

10. _____ an old horse or complain all the time

KNOW YOUR AUDIENCE

*Read the true story below, then make an inference
based on the evidence in the story.*

¹When Johannes Gutenberg invented movable type for the printing press in the 15th century, it made little difference to most people, as most people couldn't read what was being printed. ²Because most people were illiterate, it didn't make much sense to print advertisements because so few people were able to read them. ³However, William Caxton, who introduced printing into England, did print the first advertisement in English in 1472. ⁴Caxton figured that there was at least one product he could advertise and sell by use of the printed word. Can you figure out what product Caxton was selling by using a printed advertisement that few could read?

Your conclusion: _____

Which sentence has the best evidence to support your conclusion? _____

MIXED-UP CAPITALS

*Rearrange the letters below to correctly spell a capital city and its country.
Below each line are clues to the identity of the country.*

1. o o a a J T k y n p   _____, _____

   sushi, saki, Emperor Akhito, Mount Fuji, island country

2. i i i n n e a C B h g j   _____, _____

   Great Wall, 2008 Olympics, most populous country, chop suey

3. a a a a a C O t t w d n   _____, _____

   USA neighbor to the north, ice hockey, maple leaf flag

4. o a i C E r y t p g   _____, _____

   pyramids, ancient civilization, Nile River, pharaohs, hieroglyphics

5. i u e a l D n n l l r b d   _____, _____

   the Emerald Isle, leprechauns, the Blarney Stone, Gaelic

FIRST AIR RAID

Read the true story below, then make an inference
based on the evidence in the story.

[1]The first air raid in history is generally linked to the Austrians. [2]In 1849, the Austrian army had surrounded Venice and was hoping to make it surrender without a costly battle. [3]Airplanes hadn't been invented yet, but Austria knew all about balloons. [4]They attached time bombs to balloons and set them floating toward Venice, where it was expected they would blow up in the city and convince the Venetians to surrender. [5]However, things didn't work out as expected, and the first air raid is considered one of the worst military blunders in history. Can you infer what turned it into a disaster?

Your conclusion: _____

Which sentence has the best evidence to support your conclusion? _____

GEOGRAPHY RHYME TIME

hanky	Texas	Swede	mitt	Reuben	Grammy
Cuban	Norway	stallion	Lexus	Brit	deed	doorway
Finn	Miami	din	pain	Italian	Yankee	Dane

Write two rhyming words from the choice box that match the clues on each line. The first word in each set of clues has a geographic connection to the first answer word.

1. Havana sandwich   _____   _____

2. Florida music award   _____   _____

3. New England kerchief _____   _____

4. London glove   _____   _____

5. Copenhagen ache   _____   _____

6. Helsinki noise   _____   _____

7. Dallas automobile   _____   _____

8. Roman horse   _____   _____

9. Oslo entrance   _____   _____

10. Stockholm action   _____   _____

ENOUGH WITH THE NAMES

*Read the true story below, then make an inference
based on the evidence in the story.*

[1]Lake Louise, located in Banff National Park in the province of Alberta, Canada, is the world's most beautiful lake. [2]It was named in honor of the beautiful Princess Louise Caroline. [3]She was the daughter of Queen Victoria and Prince Albert of Great Britain and the wife of the governor general of Canada. [4]Princess Louise Caroline had a third name that was used to name something and yet people who live there probably don't remember where it came from. Can you infer the third name and what was named in her honor?

Your conclusion: _____

Which sentences have the best evidence to support your conclusion? _____ _____

SPEAKING HINDUSTANI

telephone	two	catalog	receipt	ferry	market
taxi		August	double	backpack	

Hindustani includes the two languages of Hindu and Urdu that are spoken the same but written differently by two population groups. Hindustani is the world's second most spoken language with about 600 million speakers.

*Write the English words from the choice box that match the Hindustani words.
Some Hindustani words are spelled incorrectly to make them easier to pronounce.*

1. do   _____

2. agast   _____

3. feree   _____

4. baazaar   _____

5. tayksee   _____

6. dabol   _____

7. fon   _____

8. raseed   _____

9. bekpek   _____

10. kaytelaag   _____

I SEE ANACREON!

Read the true story below, then make an inference
based on the evidence in the story.

[1]Anacreon was a Greek lyric poet who was born in 572 B.C. [2]This date is more than 2,000 years before the United States was founded as a nation, yet Anacreon has a strange connection to this country. [3]Anacreon's main poetic themes were love and wine, and in the 1700s, songs with those themes were called "Anacreontics." [4]Perhaps the most popular song of that era was the one entitled, "To Anacreon in Heaven." [5]Most Americans have heard the music to "To Anacreon in Heaven" more often than they have heard the music of any other song ever written. Can you infer the name of the song that was written to the music of this old English drinking song from the 1700s?

Your conclusion: _____

Which sentence has the best evidence to support your conclusion? _____

PRESIDENTIAL NAME GAME

Using the letters in the name of our third president, write smaller words
that match the definitions. The letters will always be in order either from
left to right or right to left, and may be separated by other letters.

THOMAS JEFFERSON

1.	_____	not messy, tidy
2.	_____	consume
3.	_____	follow yours to that smell
4.	_____	take it easy, relax
5.	_____	2,000 pounds
6.	_____	a male child
7.	_____	2,000 pounds backwards
8.	_____	take it to sit down
9.	_____	baby bird's home
10.	_____	long-legged water bird

I WANT A RAISE!

*Read the true story below, then make an inference
based on the evidence in the story.*

[1]Andorra is a tiny country located high in the Pyrenees Mountains between the countries of France and Spain. [2]Ever since the 13th century, Andorra has made payments to the leader of France and to the Spanish Bishop of Urgel. [3]The president of France gets about $2.00 every other year and the Bishop of Urgel gets about $8.00 every other year. [4]In addition, the bishop gets paid 6 hams, 6 cheeses, and 12 chickens every other year. [5]Can you figure out what the French leader and the Spanish bishop have been doing for the past 800 years to earn these payments?

Your conclusion: _____

Which sentence has the best evidence to support your conclusion? _____

ALL ACROSS

The letters in the word CONSTITUTION below are the first letters of words that match the clues provided. Write the missing letters in the space provided.

C_____   They make the laws.

O_____   a vow or promise

N _____   original colony, largest in the north

S _____   an address to an audience

T _____   first ten amendments

I _____   unlawful or prohibited

T _____   declared these to be self-evident

U _____   of the greatest or highest degree

T _____   fifth amendment, your right to a speedy one

I _____   to give the meaning of; to understand

O _____   person appointed or elected to office

N _____   original colony, south of Virginia

WHO DOESN'T LIKE APPLES?

*Read the true story below, then make an inference
based on the evidence in the story.*

[1]The apple tree is native to North America but these apples were "crab apples" and not nearly as large or tasty as the apples that were grown in Europe. [2]When European settlers first began settling on the east coast of North America, they brought with them apple seeds and soon were growing large and delicious apples like those grown in Europe. [3]As settlers moved west across the continent, they brought with them apple seeds to plant on their new farms and settlements. [4]However, many settlers were surprised to find apple trees already growing in areas where no settlers had ever been before. Can you infer the reason why these apple trees were growing in these unsettled areas of the west?

Your conclusion: _____

Which sentences have the best evidence to support your conclusion? _____ _____

SPEAKING DUTCH

backpack	profit	zero	snow	arrival
summer	Saturday	boat	night	sand

Dutch is the language spoken in the Netherlands. Many of the words seem familiar because both Dutch and English are in the same family of Germanic languages. About 20 million people in the world speak Dutch.

Write the English words from the choice box that best match the Dutch words below. Some Dutch words are spelled incorrectly to make them easier to pronounce.

1. nul   _____

2. Zaterdag   _____

3. zomer   _____

4. nacht   _____

5. boot   _____

6. rugzak   _____

7. aankomst   _____

8. zand   _____

9. sneeuw   _____

10. winst   _____

SOME PEOPLE JUST DON'T GET IT

Read the true story below, then make an inference
based on the evidence in the story.

[1]In past centuries, astronomical measurements weren't very exact. [2]This meant that the calendar had to be adjusted every once in awhile. [3]For instance, if the measurement of a year was off by only 6 hours, the calendar would be off by one day in only four years, ten days in 40 years, and 20 days in 80 years. [4]One of the most recent adjustments was made by King Charles IX of France in 1564. [5]The calendar had gotten so out of whack that people were celebrating New Year's Day late in March and even in early April. [6]King Charles's calendar set January 1st as New Year's Day as it is to this day. [7]However, some people refused to follow the new calendar and continued their New Year's celebrations in late March and early April. [8]Those people were called something back in the 16th century and we have set aside a day to remember them.   What special day did we set aside in their memory?

Your conclusion: _____

Which sentences have the best evidence to support your conclusion? _____   _____

WHAT'S THE RELATIONSHIP?

The words in the shaded box have a logical connection to each
other. Circle the word below the shaded box that shares the
relationship. Then explain the relationship between the words.

1. To, too, or is it two?

Congo	Lesotho	Mongolia	Togo

Mexico	Morocco	Monaco

Why? _____

2. A bee sees.

Algeria	Bolivia	Canada	Dominica

Estonia	Equador	Austria

Why? _____

3. Double trouble?

Morroco	Russia	Philippines	Seychelles

Cameroon	Andorra	Greece

Why? _____

IT SEEMS TO GO ON FOREVER

Read the true story below, then make an inference
based on the evidence in the story.

[1]The ancient Romans are credited with naming something that they may have seen but they certainly never explored. [2]In ancient times, the limit of the world, as known by the ancient Romans, was the Atlas Mountain range located at the western end of the Mediterranean Sea. [3]Anything that might be beyond those mountains was simply labeled on ancient maps as "beyond the Atlas Mountains." [4]As it turned out, this huge area "beyond the Atlas Mountains" derived its name from these mountains. Can you infer what we call this huge area today?

Your conclusion: _____

Which sentence has the best evidence to support your conclusion? _____

PRESIDENTIAL NAME GAME

Using the letters in the names of our fourth president and his wife, write smaller words that match the definitions on each line below. The letters will always be in order either from left to right or right to left, and may be separated by other letters.

JAMES & DOLLEY MADISON

1. _____   happy as Santa Claus

2. _____   earth's natural satellite

3. _____   antonym of night

4. _____   goes well with peanut butter

5. _____   What is that green stuff on the bread?

6. _____   not alive ... much like a doornail

7. _____   I'm flying all by myself!

8. _____   tall farm building for storing feed

9. _____   you made it ... you clean it up

10. _____   Hey Barbie, what did you do with Ken?

IT'S A HEMI

Read the true story below, then make an inference
based on the evidence in the story.

[1]The world globe is divided into Northern, Southern, Eastern, and Western hemispheres. [2]The area above the equator is considered the Northern Hemisphere and the land below the equator is considered the Southern Hemisphere. [3]Australia, for instance, is in the Southern Hemisphere. [4]The earliest fossil remains of humanlike creatures or "hominids" were discovered in South Africa and are called *Australopithecus* despite the fact that they were discovered thousands of miles away from Australia on a different continent entirely. Can you infer what the Latin word *australis* means?

Your conclusion: _____

Which sentences have the best evidence to support your conclusion? _____ _____

RIVER RHYME TIME

bellow	pile	Rhine	Thames	train	surrey	Rhone	Oder
cannon	Po	Shannon	snow	Nile	Seine	Murray	dine
		motor	crone	Yellow	stems		

Write two rhyming words from the choice box that match the clues below. The first word in each set of clues has a geographic connection to the first answer word.

1. Germany eat   _____   _____

2. Egypt heap   _____   _____

3. Italy precipitation   _____   _____

4. Ireland big gun   _____   _____

5. Poland engine   _____   _____

6. China river yell   _____   _____

7. England plant stalks   _____   _____

8. France railroad cars   _____   _____

9. Australia horse carriage   _____   _____

10. Switzerland old woman   _____   _____

WE HAVE TO BLAME SOMEBODY

*Read the true story below, then make an inference
based on the evidence in the story.*

[1]Some modern terms can be traced back to some long-abandoned ancient religious or cultural practice. [2]One ancient religious practice involved a high priest placing his hands on an animal and symbolically loading this poor animal down with all the people's misdeeds, mistakes, and stupidities committed in the past year. [3]The animal was blamed for every problem imaginable. [4]It was then sent off into the wilderness and nobody needed to blame themselves for their own mistakes. Can you figure out what the animal was that took the blame for the people and the modern term that still refers to this animal?

Your conclusion: _____

Which sentence has the best evidence to support your conclusion? _____

SPEAKING GREEK

candy	door	famous	pastry	boot	father
	sailors	chicken	dictionary	accident	

The Greek language is the official language of Greece. Modern Greek is a separate branch of the Indo-European family of languages. There are about 13 million Greek speakers in the world.

*Write the English words from the choice box that best match the Greek words below.
Some Greek words are spelled incorrectly to make them easier to pronounce.*

1. pateras   _____

2. porta   _____

3. naftes   _____

4. atihima   _____

5. bota   _____

6. karamela   _____

7. kotopulo   _____

8. leksiko   _____

9. fimizmenos   _____

10. filo   _____

YOU'RE NOT MAKING ANY SENSE

*Read the true story below, then make an inference
based on the evidence in the story.*

¹Babylon was one of the greatest cities of the ancient world. ²Babylon was located about 60 miles south of the present city of Baghdad, Iraq. ³The Babylonians were great builders and built the "Hanging Gardens of Babylon," famous as one of the Seven Wonders of the world. ⁴However, the Babylonians are also credited with constructing a great "ziggurat" or tower which reached so high that, according to legend, it angered the inhabitants of heaven. ⁵Apparently, the inhabitants of heaven didn't want any close neighbors. ⁶To punish the Babylonians for building this tower, the inhabitants of heaven caused those who went up it to lose the ability to make any sense when they talked. Can you infer the name of this tower and the word derived from it that refers to words that nobody can understand?

Your conclusion: _____

Which sentence has the best evidence to support your conclusion? _____

ALL ACROSS

*The letters in the word WASHINGTON below are the first letters of words that
match the clues provided. Write the missing letters in the space provided.*

W _____   Martha was his

A _____   first vice president

S _____   one who is wise and capable in governing

H _____   one known for courage and bravery

I _____   what he fought for in the Revolutionary War

N _____   a body of people sharing culture and history

G _____   his military rank

T _____   a citizen who remained loyal to the British

O _____   skillful and powerful public speaker

N _____   remarkable, worthy of notice

WHAT'S COOKING, GOOD LOOKING?

Read the true story below, then make an inference
based on the evidence in the story. .

[1]For centuries, it was the custom in France and elsewhere to roast a whole pig or ox on special holidays or for celebrations and important fairs. [2]The animal was split from "whiskers to tail" and laid on a grill over a fire and cooked until done. [3]The fire was usually composed of hickory logs as they were considered to give a special flavor to the cooking meat. [4]If you can infer the French words for "whiskers" and "tail," you can figure out what we call this kind of cooking today.

Your conclusion: _____

Which sentence has the best evidence to support your conclusion? _____

GEOGRAPHY RHYME TIME

Dutch	fleece	Peru	Missouri	tennis	trance
sand	Wales	France	tibia	billy	guru	Chile	Libya
band	Venice	flurry	sales	touch	Greece

Write two rhyming words from the choice box that match the clues below. The first word in each set of clues has a geographic connection to the first answer word.

1. Paris meditation   _____   _____

2. Tripoli leg bone   _____   _____

3. Athens wool   _____   _____

4. Italian city net game   _____   _____

5. St. Louis light snow   _____   _____

6. Netherlands contact   _____   _____

7. Welsh bargains   _____   _____

8. Sahara orchestra   _____   _____

9. Lima teacher   _____   _____

10. Santiago male goat   _____   _____

THE BULLS AND THE BEARS

Read the true story below, then make an inference
based on the evidence in the story.

[1]People all over the world refer to a "bull market" and a "bear market" without really knowing how these markets got their names. [2]If prices in a market are declining or going down, the market is called a bear market. [3]If prices in a market are rising or going up, then people call it a bull market. [4]People who believe the market will continue to rise are called "bullish" and people who believe the markets will continue to decline are called "bearish." Can you think of something that bulls and bears do when fighting that caused up and down markets to be named after them?

Your conclusion: _____

Which sentences have the best evidence to support your conclusion? _____ _____

PRESIDENTIAL NAME GAME

Using the letters in the names of our fifth president and his wife, write smaller
words that match the definitions. The letters will always be in order either
from left to right or right to left, and may be separated by other letters.

JAMES & ELIZABETH MONROE

1. _____   a park that houses many animals

2. _____   a glass container

3. _____   a wager

4. _____   to make fun of or bother

5. _____   dogs wag them

6. _____   breakfast, lunch, or dinner

7. _____   you can't have a skeleton without one

8. _____   wander about

9. _____   tardy

10. _____   confusing network of passages

PAINTING A FALSE PICTURE

*Read the true story below, then make an inference
based on the evidence in the story.*

[1]Native Americans became known as "Indians" because Christopher Columbus incorrectly assumed he had reached India. [2]The source for another misconception about Native Americans has been traced to the "Beothuk" tribe, which was almost certainly the first Native American tribe to have contact with the first European explorers along the coast of North America. [3]When the Europeans first met the Beothuk, the Beothuk were very fond of painting themselves, their clothes, their tools, and their weapons with a colored pigment. Can you infer the color of this pigment and the misconception that arose from the painting customs of the Beothuk?

Your conclusion: _____

Which sentence has the best evidence to support your conclusion? _____

WHAT'S THE RELATIONSHIP?

The words in the shaded box have a logical connection to each other. Circle the word below the shaded box that shares the relationship. Then explain the relationship between the words.

1. I'm in the middle of something here!

Canada	Huang	Danube	Shannon

Jordan   Snake   Yangtze

Why? _____

2. Does it really make a difference in the end?

Columbia	Ohio	Mackenzie	Tallahatchie

Gambia   Amazon   Tennessee

Why? _____

3. Did you end up where you began?

Oahu	Aruba	Antigua	Elba

Cuba   Attu   Malta

Why? _____

DOES THE NAME RING A BELL?

*Read the true story below, then make an inference
based on the evidence in the story.*

[1]Sir Benjamin Hall was the commissioner of public works for the city of London in the mid-19th century. [2]Sir Benjamin was taller than the average height at the time and he was kindly referred to as quite stout. [3]We can safely assume from that description that Sir Benjamin was quite a large gentleman. [4]Quite naturally, because of his size, Sir Benjamin was given an appropriate nickname. [5]Later, this same nickname was transferred over to something that was installed during Sir Benjamin's term as commissioner of public works. Can you infer the nickname? (Extra credit if you know what this nickname refers to.)

Your conclusion: _____

Which sentences have the best evidence to support your conclusion? _____ _____

SPEAKING PORTUGUESE

bus	easy	airplane	trust	book
doctor	court	soldier	travel	bag

Portuguese is a romance language that is descended from the Latin spoken by Roman soldiers. As a language, it is closely related to Spanish, French, and Italian. Portuguese is spoken by approximately 200 million people in Europe, Africa, Asia, Oceania, and South America.

Write the English words from the choice box that match the Portuguese words below. Some Portuguese words are spelled incorrectly to make them easier to pronounce.

1. aviao   _____

2. soldatoi   _____

3. soldato   _____

4. confiar   _____

5. saco   _____

6. livro   _____

7. autocarro   _____

8. tribunal   _____

9. facil   _____

10. medico   _____

I BOW TO YOUR SKILL

*Read the true story below, then make an inference
based on the evidence in the story.*

[1]The sport of bowling has been around for thousands of years. Archaeologists have uncovered a bowling game that was buried with a child that dates back to 5200 B.C. [2]Modern bowling can be traced back to the Middle Ages in Europe. [3]In England, in the 12th century, bowling became so popular that authorities became concerned that the English were not practicing another sport considered valuable during wartime and necessary for defense. [4]This other sport was considered so necessary to England's survival that England's Parliament even banned the sport of bowling for a time. Can you think of what sport was considered so important to England's survival?

Your conclusion: _____

Which sentence has the best evidence to support your conclusion? _____

ALL ACROSS

The letters in the words SUPREME COURT below are the first letters of words that match the clues provided. Write the missing letters in the space provided.

S _____ confirms the nomination

U _____ the United States formed one

P _____ justices are nominated by this person

R _____ a decision made

E _____ someone we admire due to age or experience

M _____ the greater number; more than half the votes

E _____ number of justices minus the Chief Justice

C _____ a set of facts; you may state yours

O _____ formal statement in reaching a decision

U _____ unfair, biased

R _____ to think things through, to conclude

T _____ length of time one can hold office

A PEACEFUL KINGDOM

Read the true story below, then make an inference
based on the evidence in the story.

[1]At one time in England's history, the king or queen had supreme authority. [2]The legal theory was that the king or queen was entitled to "peace" within his or her country. [3]Anyone breaking any royal law within the country was arrested for disturbing the monarch's peace. [4]However, everyone was entitled to a trial and the person who was entrusted to judge whether or not the peace had been truly disturbed was given a title that is still commonly used. [5]Today, the person holding this title may only judge minor crimes and perform various legal services such as performing a civil marriage but the title he or she holds is an ancient one. Can you infer the title of this once very powerful person?

Your conclusion: _____

Which sentences have the best evidence to support your conclusion? _____ _____

PRESIDENTIAL NAME GAME

Using the letters in the names of our sixth president and his wife, write smaller words that match the definitions. The letters will always be in order either from left to right or right to left, and may be separated by other letters.

JOHN QUINCY & LOUISA ADAMS

1. _____	wildly, crazily, insanely
2. _____	put together, or volunteer
3. _____	a pronoun meaning anybody
4. _____	24 hours makes one
5. _____	transgression, regrettable act
6. _____	visible water vapor in the air
7. _____	post office's main product
8. _____	express in words
9. _____	shelled creature, a bivalve mollusk
10. _____	the antonym of quiet

OK, IT MAY NOT BE TRUE

*Read the story below, then make an inference
based on the evidence in the story.*

[1]There is a popular holiday decoration that some believe got its name from an old Irish legend. [2]As the story goes, there was a certain Irish fellow who was such a terrible miser during his lifetime that when he died, he was not allowed in heaven. [3]He was a very tricky fellow and during his lifetime, he had also played several nasty tricks on the devil and he wasn't welcome in the devil's residence either. [4]As a result, this poor Irish fellow was forced to walk the earth carrying his lantern until the end of time. Can you infer this fellow's name and what holiday decoration bears his name?

Your conclusion: _____

Which sentence has the best evidence to support your conclusion? _____

SPEAKING TAGALOG

laundry	pajamas	market	kitchen	airplane
baby	pineapple	meat	jacket	nurse

Tagalog forms the basis of Filipino which is the national language of the Philippine Islands.

*Write the English words from the choice box that match the Tagalog words below.
Some Tagalog words are spelled incorrectly to make them easier to pronounce.*

1. eroplano _____

2. bata _____

3. londri _____

4. dyaket _____

5. kusina _____

6 merkado _____

7. karne _____

8. nars _____

9. padyama _____

10. pinya _____

I LOVE LUCY

Read the true story below, then make an inference
based on the evidence in the story.

[1]Lucy Ware Webb married Rutherford B. Hayes, the 19th president of the United States, in 1852. [2]Lucy Hayes was the first president's wife to have a college degree and she favored many of the popular causes of the time. [3]One of Lucy's innovations that has lasted since 1878 is the annual Easter Egg Roll on the White House lawn. [4]As first lady, Lucy gained a reputation as a gracious hostess except in one area where her beliefs led her to banish something from the White House and thus gain for herself the nickname of "Lemonade Lucy." Can you infer the reason why Lucy Hayes became famous as "Lemonade Lucy?"

Your conclusion: _____

Which sentence has the best evidence to support your conclusion? _____

GEOGRAPHY RHYME TIME

bongo	Berlin	crow	curb	Malay	Congo	deck
vanilla	bayou	twin	Maine	Czech	anesthesia	Manila
	Ohio	Indonesia	Idaho	delay	Serb	brain

Write two rhyming words from the choice box that match the clues below. The first word in each set of clues has a geographic connection to the first answer word.

1. African drum   _____   _____

2. Prague cards   _____   _____

3. Cleveland swamp   _____   _____

4. Java chloroform   _____   _____

5. Philippine flavor   _____   _____

6. Kuala Lumpur wait   _____   _____

7. German duplicate   _____   _____

8. Augusta cerebrum   _____   _____

9. Belgrade street edge   _____   _____

10. Boise blackbird   _____   _____

FULL SPEED AHEAD

Read the true story below, then make an inference
based on the evidence in the story.

[1]Over time, some technical terms become common words in everyday use. [2]One such expression, taken from the railroad industry, is in common use today and few remember where it began. [3]In the early days of railroading, there were no fancy electronic methods of telling trains if the track was clear ahead and it was safe to proceed at full speed. [4]The railroad industry devised a signal that was displayed at all dangerous intersections to tell the engineer if it was safe to proceed. [5]The signal was a large, round, metallic disk that was hung over the tracks. [6]If this ball-shaped disk was hanging up high where it could easily be seen, the engineer knew it was safe to proceed at full speed. What is the modern expression that is derived from this old railroad signal?

Your conclusion: _____

Which sentence has the best evidence to support your conclusion? _____

SPEAKING BENGALI

parents	cough	school	library	mother
button	sunglasses	raincoat	waiter	toothpaste

Write the English words from the choice box that match the Bengali words below.
Some Bengali words are spelled incorrectly to make them easier to pronounce.

1. laibreri   _____

2. maa   _____

3. babama   _____

4. renkoht   _____

5. skul   _____

6. tutpest   _____

7. wetar   _____

8. sanglas   _____

9. kashi   _____

10. bohtam   _____

A COOL IDEA

Read the true story below, then make an inference
based on the evidence in the story.

[1]Beginning in 1799, a new industry began in the northern states of New England that lasted for about 50 years before melting away. [2]A lively trade developed for this product between the New England states and the southern states of the United States, and it eventually became a worldwide trade. [3]This product was shipped from New England to the West Indies, South America, and even to faraway India in the early 1800s. [4]Oddly, but quite naturally, this product could only be harvested during the winter season. Can you infer what this product was?

Your conclusion: _____

Which sentence has the best evidence to support your conclusion? _____

ALL ACROSS

The first letters in the word CALIFORNIA below are the first letters of words that
match the clues provided. Write the missing letters in the space provided.

C _____   people in the state love to drive them

A _____   industry for raising crops and livestock

L _____   the largest city in the state

I _____   the lettuce that sank the Titanic

F _____   tasty meat served on a tortilla

O _____   grown naturally, without pesticides

R _____   a dried grape

N _____   Yosemite is this kind of park

I _____   a highway connecting two or more states

A _____   the main ingredient of guacamole

WHAT'S IN A NAME?

*Read the true story below, then make an inference
based on the evidence in the story.*

[1]Iceland, an island nation located in the North Atlantic Ocean, maintains a curious custom when it comes to names. [2]All Icelanders are officially called by their first names. [3]Their last names are their father's first name followed by "son" if they are male and "dottir" if they are female. [4]If the daughter marries, she retains the same name she was born with. [5]So, many Icelanders have the same name. Looking someone's name up in a phone book is almost impossible. [6]To make things easier, the phone company adds one bit of personal information after each name to narrow things down. Can you infer what is added to help further identify each Icelandic individual?

Your conclusion: _____

Which sentence has the best evidence to support your conclusion? _____

PRESIDENTIAL NAME GAME

Using the letters in the names of our seventh president and his wife, write smaller words that match the definitions on each line below. The letters will always be in order either from left to right or right to left, and may be separated by other letters.

ANDREW & RACHEL JACKSON

1. _____   a framework, or instrument of torture

2. _____   a bargain I bought at someone's garage

3. _____   stretch out and touch someone

4. _____   moisture on a yahoo mountain

5. _____   to guide the way or heavy metal

6. _____   a good explanation for bad behavior

7. _____   antonym of old

8. _____   winding part of a fishing pole

9. _____   If it keeps raining, we may need one.

10. _____   all that's left of my car after the accident.

IS SOMETHING BURNING?

Read the true story below, then make an inference
based on the evidence in the story.

[1]Nobody knows for sure when early people learned to make iron and use it to construct weapons or tools. [2]The ancient Hittites may be the first, because they were making iron 3,400 years ago. [3]People in India and China had discovered how to make iron at about the same time. [4]However, there is a mystery of history because a very few iron tools and weapons have been discovered that date back to as long as 6,000 years ago. [5]Were there some wise and ancient people 2,600 years before the Hittites who had discovered and then forgotten how to make iron? [6]A clue seems to be that the word for iron in several early languages translates to "metal from the sky." Can you infer where this 6,000-year-old iron probably came from?

Your conclusion: _____

Which sentence has the best evidence to support your conclusion? _____

SPEAKING HINDUSTANI

ballet	money	guide	ashtray	United States
walnut	conference	Ping-Pong	cherry	orange

Write the English words from the choice box that match the Hindustani words.
Some Hindustani words are spelled incorrectly to make them easier to pronounce.

1. gaaid   _____

2. kaanfrens   _____

3. amreekaa   _____

4. tebaltenis   _____

5. bayle   _____

6. eshtre   _____

7. naarangee   _____

8. akrot   _____

9. cheree   _____

10. payse   _____

THAT IS FAIRLY YOUNG

*Read the true story below, then make an inference
based on the evidence in the story.*

[1]Henry Clay, who died in 1852, was a leading American statesman for almost 50 years. [2]His many political talents were recognized early and he was elected to the Kentucky Legislature when he was only 26. [3]Three years later, he was appointed to the United States Senate from Kentucky, making him the youngest person ever to serve as a U.S. senator. [5]This is a record that will never be broken. Can you infer the reason why no younger person will ever serve as a United States senator?

Your conclusion: _____

Which sentences have the best evidence to support your conclusion? _____ _____

MONETARY RHYME TIME

yen	round	rank	schilling	dark	holler	drilling
dollar	mark	heal	pen	builder	krone	real	pound
	guilder	loopy	stone	franc	rupee	

Many different countries have their own names for their "monetary units" or better known as money.

Write two rhyming words from the choice box that match the clues below. The first word in the rhyme will always be the name of the money of the country in the clue.

1. Austria oil wells   _____   _____

2. Denmark rock   _____   _____

3. France position   _____   _____

4. Brazil get well   _____   _____

5. Germany unlit   _____   _____

6. India crazy   _____   _____

7. Japan ballpoint   _____   _____

8. Ireland circular   _____   _____

9. Netherlands carpenter _____   _____

10. Canada shout   _____   _____

GOOD TO THE LAST DROP

Read the true story below, then make an inference
based on the evidence in the story.

[1]Historians believe the coffee tree originated in what is now the modern country of Ethiopia. [2]Thus, Ethiopians were the first known coffee drinkers in the world. [3]However, it is generally acknowledged that coffee was introduced to the rest of the world by Arabs who had visited Ethiopia and liked the Ethiopian local brew. [4]According to Ethiopian legend, the unique properties of the coffee tree were first discovered by Ethiopian goat herders. [5]The goat herders noticed that their goats did something unusual after eating the leaves and berries of wild coffee trees. Can you infer what unusual thing the goats did after eating coffee leaves and berries?

Your conclusion: _____

Which sentences have the best evidence to support your conclusion? _____ _____

SPEAKING DUTCH

mouse	selfish	dictionary	field	hike
inside	pottery	government	padlock	father

Write the English words from the choice box that best match the Dutch words below.
Some Dutch words are spelled incorrectly to make them easier to pronounce.

1. woordenboek _____

2. vader _____

3. veld _____

4. overheid _____

5. trekken _____

6. binnen _____

7. muis _____

8. hangslot _____

9. keramiek _____

10. egoistisch _____

YOU MUST BE IMPORTANT

Read the true story below, then make an inference
based on the evidence in the story.

[1]In the 17th century, it became fashionable for English gentlemen to wear wigs whether they needed them or not. [2]These wigs could become quite large and not only covered the wearers' heads but could also hang down to their shoulders. [3]For awhile, you could tell how important someone was by the size of his wig. [4]Ordinary working men didn't wear wigs at all, but anyone who was above the working class usually wore one. [5]Today, the only people in England who still wear this style of wig are lawyers and judges who wear them as a matter of tradition. [6]This common expression, still used today, refers to a person who thinks of himself as important. Can you infer what this modern expression could be?

Your conclusion: _____

Which sentence has the best evidence to support your conclusion? _____

PRESIDENTIAL NAME GAME

Using the letters in the names of our eighth president, write smaller words that
match the definitions on each line below. The letters will always be in order
either from left to right or right to left, and may be separated by other letters.

MARTIN VAN BUREN

1. _____ an adult male

2. _____ thick, dark, sticky stuff

3. _____ female horse

4. _____ metal food can, or man living in Oz

5. _____ faster than a walk

6. _____ unappealing rodent larger than a mouse

7. _____ close

8. _____ brown from the sun

9. _____ a type of truck, often a mini

10. _____ scour, polish, or massage my back

OFFICER, WAS I SPEEDING?

Read the true story below, then make an inference
based on the evidence in the story.

[1]In England, all police officers are given a certain title. [2]This title is also used in the United States, but usually only in more rural areas. [3]The origin of the name is derived from, of all places, the Eastern Roman Empire, which dates back nearly 2,000 years. [4]Back in those days, the horse was an extremely valuable animal and it was an important job to be in charge of guarding and protecting the stable which housed these vital animals. [5]To emphasize the importance of this job, the Eastern Romans gave the impressive-sounding title of "Count of the Stables" to the person whose job it was to protect the horses. Can you infer the modern title given to many police officers that is derived from this title?

Your conclusion: _____

Which sentence has the best evidence to support your conclusion? _____

SPEAKING GREEK

suitcase	radio	allergy	ocean	yogurt
toothpaste	serious	drugstore	spider	waitress

Write the English words from the choice box that best match the Greek words below.
Some Greek words are spelled incorrectly to make them easier to pronounce.

1. okeanos   _____

2. farmakio   _____

3. rathio   _____

4. sovaros   _____

5. arakhn   _____

6. valitsa   _____

7. othodopasta   _____

8. servitora   _____

9. yiaurti   _____

10. aleryia   _____

FISHERMAN'S LUCK?

Read the true story below, then make an inference
based on the evidence in the story.

[1]The deepest lake in the United States is Crater Lake located in the Cascade Mountains of Oregon. [2]At its greatest depth, it is 1,932 feet deep. [3]The lake was formed about 6,600 years ago when a volcano collapsed, creating a huge bowl which gradually filled with water. [4]This bowl has no outlets and no streams that feed into it. [5]Native Americans knew about Crater Lake for thousands of years, but they never fished in it regardless of how hungry they were for fish. Can you infer the reason why Native Americans never considered Crater Lake a source for food?

Your conclusion: _____

Which sentence has the best evidence to support your conclusion? _____

ALL ACROSS

The first letters in the word LATITUDE below are the first letters of words that
match the clues provided.   Write the missing letters in the space provided.

L _____   capital of Portugal

A _____   capital of Greece

T _____   capital of Japan

I _____   largest city in Turkey

T _____   capital of Taiwan

U _____   city of movies and amusement

D _____   capital of Colorado

E _____   capital of Scotland

CALL ME A DONKEY'S UNCLE!

*Read the true story below, then make an inference
based on the evidence in the story.*

[1]Some things are called names that, at first, seem strange but do make a bit of sense when you think about it. [2]For instance, Samuel Cromption's invention got its name because it was a cross between two other inventions in the cotton-spinning industry. [3]We know that some animals cross breed and the result is a fine animal, but Cromption's invention was a type of crossbreed, too. [4]His invention was a "cross" or combination of two machines used to spin cotton into cloth. [5]The first invention was a "spinning jenny," although why it was named after a female donkey is unclear. [6]The second invention was a "water frame." Cromption's invention was a cross between the jenny and the water frame. Can you infer now what his new spinning machine was called?

Your conclusion: _____

Which sentence has the best evidence to support your conclusion? _____

SPEAKING PORTUGUESE

kill	fast	love	influenza	factory
heat	lake	home	great	jam

*Write the English words from the choice box that match the Portuguese words below.
Some Portuguese words are spelled incorrectly to make them easier to pronounce.*

1. fabrika _____

2. rapido _____

3. optimo _____

4. gripe _____

5. compota _____

6. casa _____

7. calor _____

8. madar _____

9. lago _____

10. amor _____

DO AS I DO, I GUESS

Read the true story below, then make an inference
based on the evidence in the story.

[1]Presidents have to be careful because what they do might create a tradition that other presidents may have to follow, whether they want to or not. [2]Such may be the case with William Howard Taft, who was the 27th president of the United States. [3]Back in 1910, President Taft attended a baseball game and did something at that game that every president since that time has been expected to do. Can you infer what baseball tradition dates back to President Taft in the year 1910?

Your conclusion: _____

Which sentence has the best evidence to support your conclusion? _____

PRESIDENTIAL NAME GAME

Using the letters in the names of our ninth president and his wife, write smaller words that match the definitions on each line below. The letters will always be in order either from left to right or right to left, and may be separated by other letters.

WILLIAM HENRY & ANNA HARRISON

1. _____   give a good shout

2. _____   give me a portion of that

3. _____   a beam of sunshine, perhaps

4. _____   a legal document telling who gets what

5. _____   Jack Sprat's piece

6. _____   a rabbit relative

7. _____   an antonym of peace

8. _____   female chicken

9. _____   a rise in the land but not quite a mountain

10. _____   unusual or barely cooked

LONG TIME NO SEE

*Read the true story below, then make an inference
based on the evidence in the story.*

[1]Abel Tasman, a Dutch sea captain, was one of the most famous early explorers of the South Pacific Ocean. [2]In 1642, he sailed from the island of Java to the island of Tasmania, which is named in his honor and is now an island state in Australia. [3]On that same voyage, he became the first European to sight New Zealand, which is an island nation to the east of Australia. [4]The Tasman Sea, which is that part of the Pacific Ocean that lies between Australia and New Zealand, is also named in his honor. [5]In 1642, Tasman's voyage lasted for 10 months and he sailed around the entire continent of Australia without seeing something that most people would think he would have spotted. Can you infer what Tasman didn't see during his remarkable voyage of discovery?

Your conclusion: _____

Which sentence has the best evidence to support your conclusion? _____

SPEAKING TAGALOG

surprise	waiter	drinking straw	potato	sculpture
tomato	police	switch	zoo	shampoo

*Write the English words from the choice box that match the Tagalog words below.
Some Tagalog words are spelled incorrectly to make them easier to pronounce.*

1. eskultura   _____

2. kamatis   _____

3. serbidor   _____

4. su   _____

5. suwits   _____

6. supresa   _____

7. pansipsip   _____

8. siyaampu   _____

9. pulis   _____

10. patatas   _____

DANCING IS GOOD FOR YOU

*Read the true story below, then make an inference
based on the evidence in the story.*

[1]For centuries, some Italians believed in a kind of disease they called "tarantism." [2]The victims of this odd ailment would leap in the air and run around making strange noises. [3]According to Italian legend, the only known cure for this ailment was for the victim to do a lively dance the Italians called the "tarantella." [4]This dance is still performed today, although the Italians no longer prescribe it as a cure for anything. [5]We know now that "tarantism" wasn't a disease at all but was caused by a nasty bite. Can you infer the name of the creature that did the biting?

Your conclusion: _____

Which sentence has the best evidence to support your conclusion? _____

SCRAMBLED COUNTRIES

aAusiltra	aaaCnd	tyEpg	manGeyr	eeGcre
lerldna	pnSia	haiCn	aeSidlzwnrt	siRsua

*Unscramble the words in the choice box to correctly spell the
name of a country that matches the clues below.*

1. _____ maple leaf flag, ice hockey, Montreal

2. _____ land of the pyramids, Suez Canal, pharaohs

3. _____ gave Mexico its language

4. _____ largest country in population, Beijing Olympics

5. _____ Alps mountains, cheese, watches

6. _____ only country that is also a continent

7. _____ country of the first Olympics, capital is Athens

8. _____ largest country in Europe, capital is Moscow

9. _____ Volkswagen, Mercedes, BMW, Porsche

10. _____ the Emerald Isle

A DEPRESSING CHARACTER

*Read the true story below, then make an inference
based on the evidence in the story.*

[1]Peter Ilyich Tchaikovsky, a 19th-century composer, was the first Russian composer to achieve worldwide fame for his compositions. [2]However, Tchaikovsky had a serious mental health issue. [3]He suffered from prolonged bouts of depression. [4]Not only was he depressed, he cast everyone who met him into gloom, as well. [5]His marriage in 1877 only lasted a short time, because his wife couldn't take Tchaikovsky's never-ending dark moods. [6]One bright spot in his life came when a wealthy widow, Nadezhda Von Meck, who loved his music, decided to support Tchaikovsky financially so he could work full time on his music. [7]However, knowing about Tchaikovsky's gloominess, Nadezhda wisely insisted on one condition for her support. Can you infer Nadezhda's only condition, which Tchaikovsky honored for the rest of his life?

Your conclusion: _____

Which sentence has the best evidence to support your conclusion? _____

SPEAKING BENGALI

restaurant	sunrise	two	soup	driver
express	snack	style	polo	toilet

*Write the English words from the choice box that best match the Bengali words below.
Some Bengali words are spelled incorrectly to make them easier to pronounce.*

1. dui _____

2. shurjouday _____

3. ekspres _____

4. draivar _____

5. komohd _____

6. stail _____

7. horspohlah _____

8. restohrae _____

9. naashta _____

10. sup _____

MIGHT MAKE YOU WONDER

*Read the true story below, then make an inference
based on the evidence in the story.*

[1]In 1820, it was discovered that electric current can produce a magnetic field. [2]In 1825, William Sturgeon invented an electromagnet. [3]These early discoveries soon led to the invention of the telegraph, which could send messages long distances over telegraph wires. [4]Samuel Morse invented the first working telegraph and sent the first long-distance message in 1844 using electricity. [5]The problem that might occur to you is that 1844 is long before any power plants that produced electricity were built. [6]There was no place to plug in a telegraph! Can you infer how the early telegraph was powered?

Your conclusion: _____

Which sentence has the best evidence to support your conclusion? _____

PRESIDENTIAL NAME GAME

Using the letters in the names of our tenth president and his wives, write smaller words that match the definitions on each line below. The letters will always be in order either from left to right or right to left, and may be separated by other letters.

JOHN, LETITIA & JULIA TYLER

1. _____   You are tardy again.

2. _____   Use your ears.

3. _____   my favorite Starbuck's drink

4. _____   Send it in the mail and I don't mean e-mail.

5. _____   Turn it up, I'm freezing.

6. _____   one who tells lies

7. _____   my floor has ceramic ones

8. _____   commercial fish-catching device

9. _____   not fake, it's genuine

10. _____   happiness to the world

YOU CALL THAT A ROAD?

Read the true story below, then make an inference
based on the evidence in the story.

[1]Ancient civilizations had long recognized the importance of roads for carrying goods by wagon, for communication, and for the movement of military forces. [2]As early as 1000 B.C., the Chinese had constructed roads between main population centers. [3]The ancient Persians were also major road builders and by 500 B.C., had constructed a large road network in their empire. [4]The most famous ancient road builders were the Romans, who by 200 B. C., were building roads all over the place. [5]Some of these Ancient Roman roads are still being used 2,000 years later. [6]This is because the Romans made one major improvement to their roads that the other empires failed to do. Can you figure out what this Roman improvement was?

Your conclusion: _____

Which sentences have the best evidence to support your conclusion? _____ _____

SPEAKING HINDUSTANI

flashlight	mouth	short	hat	reservation
antiseptic	circus	police	airplane	clock

Write the English words from the choice box that match the Hindustani words.
Some Hindustani words are spelled incorrectly to make them easier to pronounce.

1. mungh   _____

2. enteeseptik   _____

3. klak   _____

4. havaaeejahaaz _____

5. sarkas   _____

6. taarch   _____

7. topee   _____

8. palis   _____

9. buking   _____

10. chotaa   _____

WHAT TOOK YOU SO LONG?

Read the true story below, then make an inference
based on the evidence in the story.

[1]The first-known use of wheeled vehicles being pulled by horses dates as far back as 3500 B.C. [2]However, it was not until about 800 A.D., about 4,000 years later, that horses could be used to pull heavy loads. [3]The use of horses to pull heavy loads depended on the invention of the rigid horse collar which prevented something from happening that earlier horse harnesses failed to do. Can you infer what the rigid horse collar prevented from happening when horses pulled heavy loads?

Your conclusion: _____

Which sentence has the best evidence to support your conclusion? _____

SCRAMBLED BODIES OF WATER

liEhsgn	cPcifai	laAictnt	rrSpoiue	dDea
nIndia	eiBngr	iaiMghnc	xoMiec	icrVtaoi

Unscramble the words from the choice box to correctly spell the
name of the body of water that matches the clue below.

1. _____   largest of Great Lakes

2. _____   gulf named for USA's southern neighbor

3. _____   ocean between North America, Europe

4. _____   Chicago's Great Lake

5. _____   African lake named for British queen

6. _____   ocean named for large country

7. _____   strait separating Russia, USA

8. _____   channel between France, England

9. _____   world's largest ocean

10. _____   salty sea, lowest point on earth

JUST TUMBLING ALONG

*Read the true story below, then make an inference
based on the evidence in the story.*

[1]Early settlers to the Plains States were amused by the sight of "tumbleweeds" blowing around their farms during the winter season. [2]The tumbleweed is a common name for several plants, all with rounded tops, that become brittle in the fall, break off from the ground, and then blow wherever the wind takes them. [3]Watching these plants blow about on a windy winter day might have provided entertainment for families. [4]However, the early farmers soon grew to detest these amusing tumbleweeds when they discovered what purpose was being served by all this blowing about. Can you figure out the reason early farmers learned to hate the tumbling tumbleweeds?

Your conclusion: _____

Which sentence has the best evidence to support your conclusion? _____

SPEAKING DUTCH

cantaloupe	child	sugar	burn	tiny
mother	ancient	weather	borrow	sunny

*Write the English words from the choice box that match the Dutch words below.
Some Dutch words are spelled incorrectly to make them easier to pronounce.*

1. suiker   _____

2. zonnig   _____

3. miniem   _____

4. weer   _____

5. branden   _____

6. oud   _____

7. lenen   _____

8. meleon   _____

9. kind   _____

10. moeder   _____

A MAGIC MARKER?

*Read the true story below, then make an inference
based on the evidence in the story.*

[1]Samuel Langhorne Clemens is one of America's most famous authors, although he is better known by his pen name of "Mark Twain." [2]Some of his most famous books include "The Adventures of Huckleberry Finn" and "The Adventures of Tom Sawyer." [3]At one time in his life, Clemens was a riverboat pilot on the Mississippi River and it was from this experience that he chose his pen name. [4]The term "mark twain" was a common term used on riverboats of the time. Can you infer what they were "marking" when they used the term "mark twain?"

Your conclusion: _____

Which sentence has the best evidence to support your conclusion? _____

PRESIDENTIAL NAME GAME

Using the letters in the names of our eleventh president and his wife, write smaller words that match the definitions on each line below. The letters will always be in order either from left to right or right to left, and may be seprated by other letters.

JAMES KNOX & SARAH POLK

1. _____   a playful or mischievous act

2. _____   type of music or knock on door

3. _____   a verse written by a poet

4. _____   a blemish or your grade

5. _____   Do this for your picture.

6. _____   Do this before you leap or cross street.

7. _____   a tree that grows from an acorn

8. _____   be happy as this small songbird

9. _____   Go play in one.

10. _____   Don't cause this damage to anyone.

DANCING WITH A PURPOSE

Read the true story below, then make an inference
based on the evidence in the story.

[1]We know that dancing was one of the earliest forms of artistic and religious expression, because we have found pictures of humans dancing on wall paintings in caves that are 20,000 years old. [2]We know dancing was important to Ancient Egyptians, because they have left us paintings, sculptures, and writings detailing their dances. [3]Different groups of Egyptians danced in honor of different gods who were thought to be in charge of different aspects of Egyptian life, although everyone honored all the gods. [4]For instance, Egyptian farmers danced most fervently in honor of the Egyptian god "Osiris." Can you infer what Osiris was thought to be responsible for in Egypt?

Your conclusion: _____

Which sentence has the best evidence to support your conclusion? _____

SPEAKING GREEK

rice	soup	bad	perfume	castle
cookie	scalp	sandal	number	baseball

Write the English words from the choice box that best match the Greek words below.
Some Greek words are spelled incorrectly to make them easier to pronounce.

1. kakos _____

2. biskoto _____

3. beizbol _____

4. kastro _____

5. arithmos _____

6. aroma _____

7. rizi _____

8. sadali _____

9. kranio _____

10. supa _____

DON'T DRINK THE WATER

Read the true story below, then make an inference
based on the evidence in the story.

[1]There is a saltwater lake in Asia that is very unusual. [2]For one thing, it is called a "sea" instead of a lake, which is what it is. [3]For another thing, it is the saltiest body of water in the world and is nine times saltier than the oceans. [4]For still another thing, the shore of this lake or sea is 1,310 feet below sea level, which makes it the lowest point on the surface of the earth. [5]Finally, no fish live in this lake and barely any plants live in it or even near it. Can you infer the name of this strange lake or sea?

Your conclusion: _____

Which sentence has the best evidence to support your conclusion? _____

RHYME TIME

soccer	fountain	king	gravies	tart	Sphinx
notion	mountain	locker	bees	debater	ocean	navy's
shivers	bling	sea's	chart	river's	equator	drinks

Write two rhyming words from the choice box that match the clues below.

1. alpine waterworks   _____   _____

2. sea idea   _____   _____

3. imaginary line arguer   _____   _____

4. monarch showy items   _____   _____

5. Mississippi's chills   _____   _____

6. fleet's sauces   _____   _____

7. Mediterranean's insects   _____   _____

8. map small pie   _____   _____

9. football warehouse   _____   _____

10. mythological beast sodas _____   _____

BEWARE OF THE MOTH!

*Read the true story below, then make an inference
based on the evidence in the story.*

¹Every culture has its own superstitions and beliefs that don't seem to have a common-sense source. ²This is not the case with the superstitions that have arisen concerning one type of moth found in Africa and southern parts of Europe. ³This moth has a thick, hairy body, likes to enter beehives and dine on honey, and if it is disturbed, it may make a loud, squeaking noise. ⁴However, what gives rise to a common superstition in both Europe and Africa is the pattern or markings on the moth's body, which look very much like the skull of a long-dead human. ⁵The common superstition is that the moth's appearance foretells the death of someone. Can you infer the common name of this moth based on this superstition and the markings on its body?

Your conclusion: _____

Which sentence has the best evidence to support your conclusion? _____

SPEAKING PORTUGUESE

necklace	singer	past	oven	market
room	matches	shampoo	rope	permission

*Write the English words from the choice box that match the Portuguese words below.
Some Portuguese words are spelled incorrectly to make them easier to pronounce.*

1. mercado   _____

2. fosforos   _____

3. colar   _____

4. forno   _____

5. passado   _____

6. licenca   _____

7. quarto   _____

8. corda   _____

9. cantor   _____

10. champo   _____

WE HONOR THEM ALL

*Read the true story below, then make an inference
based on the evidence in the story.*

[1]The United States awards medals and decorations to people who have performed deeds of bravery or who have contributed distinguished service to the nation. [2]If the decoration is in the form of a star or cross, the person showed heroism in battle. [3]A round medal indicates the person gave distinguished service either during peace or war. [4]The Purple Heart is, of course, heart shaped and is awarded only to those members of the military who were wounded or killed in combat. [5]The Purple Heart also has the face of George Washington on it. Can you figure out why George Washington's face appears on the Purple Heart?

Your conclusion: _____

Which sentence has the best evidence to support your conclusion? _____

PRESIDENTIAL NAME GAME

Using the letters in the names of our twelfth president and his wife, write smaller words that match the definitions on each line below. The letters will always be in order either from left to right or right to left, and may be separated by other letters.

ZACHARY & MARGARET TAYLOR

1. _____   map or plan a course

2. _____   to wed

3. _____   solemn vow or promise

4. _____   to transport or keep in stock

5. _____   a salty eye drop or a rip

6. _____   elected head of a city

7. _____   shining circle around head

8. _____   decay

9. _____   drab color spelled two ways

10. _____   365 days

MADE TO LAST

Read the true story below, then make an inference
based on the evidence in the story.

¹In these modern times, we are familiar with many different fabrics. ²One fabric that we are familiar with has been around for far longer that we probably realize. ³This sturdy fabric has been woven for at least 1,700 years and is still going strong today. ⁴This fabric originated in the town of Nimes, France, and was known as "serge de Nimes" for many centuries. Can you infer what we call this still popular fabric today?

Your conclusion: _____

Which sentence has the best evidence to support your conclusion? _____

SPEAKING TAGALOG

goose	desert	patient	newspaper	gnat
drapes	luggage	intersection	fruit	library

Write the English words from the choice box that match the Tagalog words below.
Some Tagalog words are spelled incorrectly to make them easier to pronounce.

1. pasyente _____

2. peryodiko _____

3. bagahe _____

4. librereya _____

5. krosing _____

6. gansa _____

7. niknik _____

8. prutas _____

9. kurtina _____

10. disyerto _____

A CLEVER WOMAN

Read the story below, then make an inference
based on the evidence in the story.

[1]When faced with a problem in ancient times, the mythological heroes and heroines often found clever solutions. [2]One such case is in the legend of "Dido," the founder and first queen of the city of Carthage in Africa. [3]Carthage was one of the greatest cities of the ancient world and, for a time, was Rome's chief rival. [4]Dido fled to Africa, as the story goes, to escape from her murderous brother. [5]When she landed in Africa, the rulers only offered her as much land as might be outlined by the hide of a bull they gave her. Can you infer what clever solution Dido came up with to make the outline of that bull's hide large enough to create the city of Carthage?

Your conclusion: _____

Which sentence has the best evidence to support your conclusion? _____

BEFORE AND AFTER

Caesar	Liberty	Memorial	Mountain	Pole
Washington	Light	New York	Belgium	Gettysburg

Write the word from the choice box that makes sense in the blank between
the two words or sets of words below. Use each choice box word once.

1. Rocky   _____   Dew

2. George   _____   Monument

3. North   _____   vault

4. Battle of   _____   Address

5. City of   _____   bulb

6. Julius   _____   salad

7. Brussels   _____   waffle

8. Statue of   _____   Bell

9. Albany   _____   Yankees

10. Lincoln   _____   Day

EASY COME AND EASY GO

Read the true story below, then make an inference
based on the evidence in the story.

[1]There is one thing we probably use every day and maybe even several times a day that was first made way back in the year 1519. [2]It was made in the St. Joachim's Valley in an area known as Bohemia in Europe. [3]At first, it was given the rather imposing name of *Joachimsthaler*. [4]This tongue-twister of a name was later rather sensibly shortened to just "thaler." [5]Still later, when we began using it, we changed the name even more. Can you infer what we call the original *Joachimsthaler* today?

Your conclusion: _____

Which sentences have the best evidence to support your conclusion? _____ _____

PRESIDENTIAL NAME GAME

Using the letters in the names of our thirteenth president and his wives, write smaller words that match the definitions on each line below. The letters will always be in order either from left to right or right to left, and may be separated by other letters.

MILLARD, ABIGAIL & CAROLINE FILLMORE

1. _____   use the telephone

2. _____   a movie

3. _____   warning that a burglar is busy

4. _____   separate space in a house

5. _____   physical effort, like giving birth

6. _____   1,000,000

7. _____   green citrus fruit

8. _____   a Christmas song

9. _____   be unsuccessful on a test

10. _____   old-fashioned way to use a telephone

SEEMS A BIT OVER THE TOP

Read the true story below, then make an inference
based on the evidence in the story.

[1]Draco was an ancient Greek lawmaker who introduced the first written code of law in Athens in 621 B.C. [2]Until Draco came along, the laws were pretty much whatever the judges said they were. [3]This system was basically unfair, because nobody really knew for sure what was against the law, as it was all in the judges' heads. [4]So, Draco did a good thing, but his name is used in the word "Draconian," which means harsh or cruel. [5]Draco's good deed is thus rewarded with his name being associated with harshness for more that 2,000 years. Can you figure out what was in Draco's law code that caused his name to be associated with harshness and cruelty throughout the centuries?

Your conclusion: _____

Which sentence has the best evidence to support your conclusion? _____

SPEAKING BENGALI

coffee	doctor	dessert	luggage	engine
ice cream	apple	airline	bicycle	bakery

Write the English words from the choice box that best match the Bengali words below.
Some Bengali words are spelled incorrectly to make them easier to pronounce.

1. dezart   _____

2. oopel   _____

3. daktar   _____

4. earline   _____

5. bagej   _____

6. bekari   _____

7. saikel   _____

8. kofi   _____

9. injin   _____

10. aiskrim   _____

SIGN ON THE DOTTED LINE

*Read the true story below, then make an inference
based on the evidence in the story.*

[1]People buy accident insurance to limit their risk in case of an accident. [2]You pay a fee and the insurance company shares the cost of paying for any accidents that you may have. [3]There is a word the insurance industry uses to describe this activity of issuing insurance policies to share the risk [4]This word dates back to England in the 1600s, when ship owners would pay a fee to wealthy individuals who would share the risk of ships and cargoes being lost at sea. [5]If the ships sank, the wealthy individuals would pay part of the ship owners' losses. [6]The first insurance polices were simple documents which listed the ship and its cargo at the top with space below for the signatures of the wealthy people who were sharing the risk with the ship owner. [7]From the design of this simple document, we get a word that is now used to describe issuing insurance policies. Can you infer the word?

Your conclusion: _____

Which sentences have the best evidence to support your conclusion? _____ _____

ALL ACROSS

The letters in the word VIRGINIA below are the first letters of words that match the clues provided. Write the missing letters in the space provided.

V _____   deer meat, eaten by early settlers

I _____   one of the first

R _____   the capital city

G _____   His home is named Mt. Vernon.

I _____   Native Americans, the first inhabitants

N _____   the state on the southern border

I _____   Colonists felt this way at being taxed without representation.

A _____   borders this ocean

GONE BUT NOT FORGOTTEN

Read the true story below, then make an inference
based on the evidence in the story.

[1]According to ancient Greek and Roman mythology, Uranus was the name of the earliest god of the sky. [2]His function was taken over by his grandson, who was called Zeus by the Greeks and Jupiter by the Romans. [3]In 1781, the British astronomer Sir William Hershel discovered the seventh planet from the sun. [4]He decided to name it after this almost forgotten ancient god of the sky and called this new planet Uranus. [5]Everyone was still excited by this discovery of an undiscovered planet when a German chemist, Martin H. Klapnoth, discovered a new element in 1789. Can you infer what Klapnoth named his new element?

Your conclusion: _____

Which sentence has the best evidence to support your conclusion? _____

PRESIDENTIAL NAME GAME

Using the letters in the names of our fourteenth president and his wife, write smaller
words that match the definitions on each line below, The letters will always be in
order either from left to right or right to left, and may be separated by other letters.

FRANKLIN & JANE PIERCE

1. _____   a part of the whole, like a slice of pie

2. _____   another name for wharf or dock

3. _____   Paris is its capital

4. _____   an ache

5. _____   a bent lever you turn, or strange person

6. _____   popular grain, especially in China

7. _____   water from the sky

8. _____   flesh around the mouth

9. _____   fruit that is ready to pick

10. _____   joint between your foot and leg

VIKING'S BEST FRIEND?

Read the true story below, then make an inference
based on the evidence in the story.

[1]For thousands of years, humans have used dogs for protection, in hunting, and in caring for livestock. [2]The Vikings, who were fierce warriors and sailors, developed a special relationship with the raven. [3]It was a favorite symbol of the Vikings and was depicted on Viking flags. [4]The Vikings were the first Europeans to take long ocean voyages and even ventured across the Atlantic Ocean to visit America long before anyone else. [5]The Vikings always made sure to take ravens with them when they made their long ocean voyages for a very practical reason. Can you infer what the Vikings used the ravens for on their long ocean voyages far from land?

Your conclusion: _____

Which sentences have the best evidence to support your conclusion? _____ _____

SPEAKING HINDUSTANI

enter	blackberry	tour	ambulance	new
papaya	center	highway	liver	plate

Write the English words from the choice box that match the Hindustani words below.
Some Hindustani words are spelled incorrectly to make them easier to pronounce.

1. embulens _____

2. kendra _____

3. dauraa _____

4. nayaa _____

5. plet _____

6. motarvee _____

7. andarjaanaa _____

8. jigar _____

9. papeetaa _____

10. kaleeberee _____

EIGHT IS ENOUGH

*Read the true story below, then make an inference
based on the evidence in the story.*

[1]One of the United States has curiously become associated with the number 8. [2]It is called the "Mother of Presidents" because eight presidents were born there. [3]It is also called the "Mother of States" because the states of Illinois, Indiana, Kentucky, Michigan, Minnesota, Ohio, West Virginia, and Wisconsin were formed in whole, or in part, from western territory once claimed by this state. [4]Finally, this state has exactly 8 letters in its name. Can you infer the name of this state?

Your conclusion: _____

Which sentence has the best evidence to support your conclusion? _____

BEFORE AND AFTER

Stone	Rose	White	David	Hill
Columbus	King	Bull	Tower	English

*Write the word from the choice box that makes sense in the blank between
the two words or set of words below. Use each choice box word once.*

1. Snow   _____   House

2. Christopher   _____   Ohio

3. Compass   _____   bush

4. Martin Luther _____   of hearts

5. Camp   _____   Beckham

6. Sitting   _____   fight

7. Standard   _____   Channel

8. Eiffel   _____   of London

9. Blarney   _____   Henge

10. Bunker   _____   of beans

HOT STUFF?

Read the story below, then make an inference
based on the evidence in the story.

[1]In Roman mythology, Vulcan was the god of fire. [2]He was considered the blacksmith to the gods and used his mastery of fire to create weapons and tools for the gods. [3]Vulcan was the only major god to have a physical handicap, as he was lame. [4]Despite his handicap, Vulcan was married to Venus, who was the goddess of love and beauty. [5]Venus may not have always been faithful to Vulcan, but that is another story. [6]Vulcan is mainly remembered today because his name was the basis for naming a common phenomenon involving fire. Can you infer what was named for Vulcan?

Your conclusion: _____

Which sentence has the best evidence to support your conclusion? _____

SPEAKING DUTCH

mud	peanut	wallet	nose	hammock
intermission	puncture	towel	wash	salt

Write the English words from the choice box that match the Dutch words below.
Some Dutch words are spelled incorrectly to make them easier to pronounce.

1. neus   _____

2. pinda   _____

3. lek   _____

4. zout   _____

5. handoek   _____

6. portemonnee   _____

7. wassen   _____

8. hangmat   _____

9. pause   _____

10. modder   _____

IT 'SODA' MAKES SENSE

*Read the true story below, then make an inference
based on the evidence in the story.*

[1]Carbonated soft drinks date back to 1772, when an English chemist, Joseph Priestly, used soda to carbonate water. [2]Priestly's carbonated water became known as "soda water." [3]Later, others added fruit juices to this soda water and in the 1800s, people were buying these drinks at "soda fountains." [4]In about 1850, people started adding the word "pop" to soda water and before long, everyone was talking about drinking "soda pop." [5]Today, if someone offers you a glass of pop, you know they are offering you a carbonated soft drink of some kind. Can you infer what happened in 1850 to cause people to start adding the word pop to the word soda?

Your conclusion: _____

Which sentence has the best evidence to support your conclusion? _____

PRESIDENTIAL NAME GAME

Using the letters in the names of our fifteenth president, who was our only bachelor president, and his niece, write smaller words that match the definitions on each line below. The letters will always be in order either from left to right or right to left, and may be separated by other letters.

JAMES BUCHANAN & HARRIET LANE

1. _____   cross between a donkey and horse

2. _____   strait between England, France

3. _____   container made of wood that holds liquid

4. _____   to be introduced to

5. _____   pleasing to others

6. _____   long yellow fruit

7. _____   part of the wheel on a car

8. _____   your side in a game

9. _____   Ouch! That's hot! I hurt myself!

10. _____   candy treat or walking stick

IS THAT YOUR DOG?

*Read the true story below, then make an inference
based on the evidence in the story.*

[1]The "spaniel" is the common name for quite a large family of related dogs, most of them bred and named for different parts of the British Isles. [2]The American Kennel Club recognizes 10 different spaniel breeds. [3]Among them are the American Water, Clumber, Cocker, English Cocker, English Springer, Field Irish, Sussex, and the Welsh Springer. [4]All spaniels were originally hunting dogs, but today, the vast majority of them are simply family pets. [5]Experts believe that all spaniels are descended from a dog first bred in one country. Can you infer the name of this country?

Your conclusion: _____

Which sentence has the best evidence to support your conclusion? _____

ALL ACROSS

The letters in the words VALLEY FORGE below are the first letters of words that match the clues provided. Write the missing letters in the space provided.

V_____   How cold was it?

A_____   a military force, not the navy

L_____   General Washington was this to his men

L_____   to put a boat into the water

E_____   The army slept in tents here.

Y_____   despite hardship, the men refused to do this

F_____   many men's fingers and toes were affected

O_____   very difficult, stressful situation

R_____   Which war was it?

G_____   first name of the general

E_____   They did this despite the lack of food and warm clothing.

TOUGH ORAL QUIZ

*Read the story below, then make an inference
based on the evidence in the story.*

[1]The most famous Sphinx is probably the one located in Giza, Egypt. [2]However, other Near East and Greek cultures had their own versions of this mythical creature. [3]In the Greek myth, the Sphinx lived on a high rock near the city of Thebes and stopped anyone who passed by. [4]The Sphinx would give these travelers a riddle. [5]If they solved the riddle, they were allowed to pass safely. If they couldn't solve the riddle, they were tossed off the rock and killed. [6]The riddle was, "What has one voice and becomes four-footed, two-footed, and then three-footed?" Can you answer the riddle or will you be tossed off the mountain by the Sphinx?

Your conclusion: _____

Which sentence has the best evidence to support your conclusion? _____

SPEAKING GREEK

night	tomato	stairway	library	wind
watch	tea	science	map	shampoo

*Write the English words from the choice box that best match the Greek words below.
Some Greek words are spelled incorrectly to make them easier to pronounce.*

1. skala _____

2. tsai _____

3. domata _____

4. roloi _____

5. anemos _____

6. sampuan _____

7. epistimi _____

8. nikhta _____

9. khartis _____

10. vivliothiki _____

THE FACE IS FAMILIAR

Read the true story below, then make an inference
based on the evidence in the story.

[1]Some people become so famous that their faces are recognized by billions of people. [2]However, one person's face is recognized by billions of people all around the world, yet only a very few know her name. [3]This face belongs to a rather humble wife and mother by the name of Charlotte Bartholdi. [4]Her face has been reproduced millions of times in coins, posters, paintings, stamps, films, and countless photographs. [5]Millions more have personally visited Charlotte's face reproduced in a huge fashion. [6]Obviously, Charlotte's face was used as a model for something very famous, but can you figure out what this is?

Your conclusion: _____

Which sentences have the best evidence to support your conclusion? _____ _____

PRESIDENTIAL NAME GAME

Using the letters in the names of our sixteenth president and his wife, write smaller words that match the definitions on each line below. The letters will always be in order either from left to right or right to left, and may be separated by other letters.

ABRAHAM & MARY TODD LINCOLN

1. _____   a weaving machine

2. _____   a spoiled child or sausage

3. _____   a useful device, like a screwdriver

4. _____   strange or number not divisible evenly by 2

5. _____   difficult or not soft

6. _____   home for livestock

7. _____   a baby sheep

8. _____   limb that ends with a hand

9. _____   a shopping center

10. _____   fee for using a road

LET'S HAVE A RACE

*Read the true story below, then make an inference
based on the evidence in the story.*

[1]One type of race that today is both a track and field competition and a race conducted on horseback, dates back to the 1700s in Ireland. [2]According to legend, two men were out riding their horses in the countryside and decided to race their horses in a straight line to the nearest man-made structure they could see. [3]This meant they would have to jump whatever obstacles that were in their way, such as streams, hedges, or fences, as they raced to the landmark. [4]This exciting type of racing became very popular and soon racetracks were placing different obstacles on the track and people were betting for their favorites. [5]The name for this event came from the fact that the two men who originated the race were trying to get to the local church's bell tower as the finish line. Can you infer the name we use for this type of racing?

Your conclusion: _____

Which sentence has the best evidence to support your conclusion? _____

BEFORE AND AFTER

plates	tip	Cape	flakes	Court
General	Rock	table	home	pie

*Write the word from the choice box that makes sense in the blank between
the two words or sets of words below. Use each choice box word once.*

1. Plymouth   _____   and roll

2. Attorney   _____   Motors

3. Tennis   _____   of Appeals

4. Ping-Pong   _____   of contents

5. Pumpkin   _____   chart

6. Foul   _____   toes

7. Corn   _____   of snow

8. Tectonic   _____   of food

9. Ranch style   _____   of the brave

10. Batman's   _____   Cod

THAT IS A TALL STORY

*Read the story below, then make an inference
based on the evidence in the story.*

[1]Many Americans are familiar with the American folk tale about Paul Bunyan and Babe, the Blue Ox. [2]A lesser-known American folk tale concerns a gigantic sea captain named Alfred Bulltop Stormalong. [3]His ship was so big his crew had to ride horseback to get from one end to the other. [4]Sailors sent to climb the riggings as young men took so long, they returned with long, gray beards. [5]He had to soap the sides of his ship to squeeze it through the English Channel and when the soap scraped off, he had created the White Cliffs of Dover. [6]The masts of his ship were constructed with hinges, so they could be folded down when necessary. Can you infer the reason why Captain Stormalong had to fold his masts?

Your conclusion: _____

Which sentence has the best evidence to support your conclusion? _____

SPEAKING PORTUGUESE

voice	sun	king	tooth	shape
yellow	wash	throat	speed	tweezers

*Write the English words from the choice box that match the Portuguese words below.
Some Portuguese words are spelled incorrectly to make them easier to pronounce.*

1. forma _____

2. velocidade _____

3. garganta _____

4. sol _____

5. voz _____

6. lavor _____

7. pinca _____

8. amarelo _____

9. dente _____

10. rei _____

RED AND WHITE AND READ ALL OVER?

*Read the true story below, then make an inference
based on the evidence in the story.*

[1]In Europe during the Middle Ages, there was a narrow line separating the work of a barber and that of a surgeon. [2]Both professions performed surgical operations, but the principal job of "bloodletting" was generally left to barbers to perform. [3]In those days, many illnesses were treated by draining blood from patients in the hope of getting rid of the "bad blood" causing the illness. [4]To advertise this bloodletting service, barbers began placing outside their shops the traditional red-and-white-striped barber poles still used today by barbers. [5]The red stripe on the barber pole stands for blood but can you infer what the white stripe represents?

Your conclusion: _____

Which sentence has the best evidence to support your conclusion? _____

PRESIDENTIAL NAME GAME

Using the letters in the names of our seventeenth president and his wife, write smaller words that match the definitions on each line below. The letters will always be in order either from left to right or right to left, and may be separated by other letters.

ANDREW & ELIZA JOHNSON

1. _____ smoke or vapor in the air or to harass, abuse

2. _____ mouth bone

3. _____ It's twelve and time for lunch.

4. _____ large wild cat and king of the jungle

5. _____ the purpose for doing something

6. _____ plant part that the farmer plants

7. _____ what you did to get a picture

8. _____ dirt

9. _____ fly upward, like an eagle

10. _____ marry

A BIG WHEEL

Read the true story below, then make an inference
based on the evidence in the story.

[1]There is a common entertainment device and tourist attraction that was originally called a "pleasure wheel." [2]It was always called that until a mechanical engineer built a pleasure wheel for the World's Columbian Exposition held in Chicago, Illinois, in 1893. [3]The pleasure wheel this engineer designed was so large it could carry 2,160 people on it at one time. Can you infer this mechanical engineer's last name?

Your conclusion: _____

Which sentence has the best evidence to support your conclusion? _____

SPEAKING TAGALOG

cake	tea	cookie	bathroom	soap
hat	book	address	crime	bandage

Write the English words from the choice box that match the Tagalog words below.
Some Tagalog words are spelled incorrectly to make them easier to pronounce.

1. biskwit _____

2. krimen _____

3. keyk _____

4. libro _____

5. banyo _____

6. direksiyon _____

7. benda _____

8. sabon _____

9. sumbrero _____

10. tsaa _____

NUMBER, PLEASE

*Read the true story below, then make an inference
based on the evidence in the story.*

[1]Leonardo Fibonacci was an Italian mathematician who helped introduce Hindu-Arabic numerals to Europe in the 13th century. [2]These are the numbers 0,1,2,3,4,5,6,7,8, and 9 that we are all familiar with today. [3]But Fibonacci is best known today for inventing a special series of numbers known as the "Fibonacci Sequence" that was much-studied by mathematicians over the centuries and is still studied today. [4]The Fibonacci Sequence starts 1,1,2,3,5,8,13 and so on using the same formula over and over again. [5]If you can deduce the next number after 13 in the Fibonacci Sequence, then you will understand its basic principle. What number comes after 13?

Your conclusion: _____

Which sentence has the best evidence to support your conclusion? _____

SCRAMBLED MAJOR CITIES

onLisb	saWwar	mbayBo	lskiHein	aianghSh
anavaH	rakAan	gtoninWell	eutirB	daBustpe

*Unscramble the words in the choice box to correctly spell
the name of a major that matches the clue below.*

1. _____   capital of Finland

2. _____   India's most populous city

3. _____   capital of Cuba

4. _____   China's most populous city

5. _____   capital of Hungary

6. _____   capital of Lebanon

7. _____   capital of New Zealand

8. _____   capital of Poland

9. _____   capital of Portugal

10. _____   capital of Turkey

A REMINDER FROM HOME

Read the true story below, then make an inference
based on the evidence in the story.

[1]During World War II, so many millions of letters were sent by wives and girlfriends to husbands and boyfriends serving in the military that the post office was overwhelmed. [2]To solve this problem, "V-mail" was invented. [3]It was a one-page form, so wives and girlfriends could write on one page only. [4]This page was then sent through a machine to be photographed. Each roll of film could hold thousands of V-mails. [5]Later, the film was developed overseas at a processing center and the letter reproduced and sent on to the military man. [6]The major problem with this system occurred at the machine that photographed the V-mails. [7]Something kept gumming up the works and workers had to frequently stop the operation and clean the machine. [8]They referred to this as the "scarlet scourge." Can you infer what they meant by the scarlet scourge?

Your conclusion: _____

Which sentences have the best evidence to support your conclusion? _____ _____

PRESIDENTIAL NAME GAME

Using the letters in the names of our eighteenth president and his wife, write smaller words that match the definitions on each line below. The letters will always be in order either from left to right or right to left, and may be separated by other letters.

ULYSSES SIMPSON & JULIA GRANT

1. _____   someone who secretly gathers information

2. _____   fail to hit or an unmarried girl

3. _____   breathe hard like a dog

4. _____   to bring up or lift

5. _____   antonym of no

6. _____   a meeting of jazz musicians

7. _____   drink a tiny amount

8. _____   wash with water only

9. _____   a person who fibs

10. _____   smaller amount than others received

PLEASED TO MEET YOU?

*Read the true story below, then make an inference
based on the evidence in the story.*

[1]Revolutionary inventions often present people with odd problems when they are first put to use. [2]For instance, after Alexander Graham Bell invented the telephone, people were presented with the problem of what to say when they answered it. [3]Bell suggested people should say "AHOY" when they first spoke into the telephone. [4]The great inventor, Thomas Edison, thought he had a better word that he suggested people say when they answered the telephone. Can you infer what new word Thomas Edison invented for people to say when answering the telephone?

Your conclusion: _____

Which sentence has the best evidence to support your conclusion? _____

SPEAKING BENGALI

tin can	contest	traffic	heart	wool
long	hat	classical	walking trail	diary

*Write the English words from the choice box that best match the Bengali words below.
Some Bengali words are spelled incorrectly to make them easier to pronounce.*

1. klasikal   _____

2. hart   _____

3. tupi   _____

4. lomba   _____

5. teen   _____

6. ul   _____

7. mach   _____

8. dairi   _____

9. futpat   _____

10. trqfik   _____

CHANGE IS GOOD

*Read the true story below, then make an inference
based on the evidence in the story.*

[1]In the early days of our country, the Spanish peso or "piece of eight" was widely used because the value was in the precious metal used to make the coin. [2]This coin was often cut into as many as eight smaller pieces because everything didn't cost as much as a full-sized coin. [3]For instance, a loaf of bread might only cost one bit or piece of a full-sized coin or a sack of beans might only cost three bits or pieces of the piece of eight. [4]A slang word we use today for one of our coins is a relic from the old days when we cut coins into smaller pieces. Can you infer the name of the modern coin that should remind us of the days when coins were cut into pieces?

Your conclusion: _____

Which sentence has the best evidence to support your conclusion? _____

SPEAKING HINDUSTANI

eight	Spain	hockey	fingernail	warm
wool	corner	office	thermometer	shuttle

*Write the English words from the choice box that match the Hindustani words below.
Some Hindustani words are spelled incorrectly to make them easier to pronounce.*

1. garm   _____

2. Spen   _____

3. temameetar _____

4. aafis   _____

5. nel   _____

6. haakee   _____

7. kanaa   _____

8. shatal   _____

9. aat   _____

10. oon   _____

MY BODY LIES OVER THE OCEAN

Read the true story below, then make an inference
based on the evidence in the story.

¹One place in the Atlantic Ocean is so dangerous that it has earned a deathly title. ²Cape Hatteras sticks out from the southern tip of Hatteras Island. ³The island itself lies some 30 miles east of the North Carolina coast, amid underwater reefs called the Diamond Shoals. ⁴Many shipwrecks have occurred in this area and enough sailors have lost their lives in these dangerous waters to fill several cemeteries ⁵This has resulted in earning this area a special four-word title. ⁶The last three words of this title are "of the Atlantic." Can you infer the appropriate first word of this four-word title?

Your conclusion: _____

Which sentence has the best evidence to support your conclusion? _____

PRESIDENTIAL NAME GAME

Using the letters in the names of our nineteenth president and his wife, write smaller words that match the definitions on each line below. The letters will always be in order either from left to right or right to left, and may be separated by other letters.

RUTHERFORD BIRCHARD & LUCY HAYES

1. _____ wade across a river or maybe an automobile

2. _____ grove of apple or cherry trees

3. _____ to give a job to

4. _____ 3 feet or 36 inches

5. _____ place after second

6. _____ wealthy

7. _____ dried grass often piled in stacks

8. _____ bark used to make canoes

9. _____ what a ruler does or a law

10. _____ to purchase

A SIGN OF A DOG?

Read the true story below, then make an inference
based on the evidence in the story.

[1]If you come across a "Beware of the Dog" sign, you know this is a warning you should pay attention to. [2]Credit for the first dog-warning signs goes to the ancient Romans, who used to post signs that said *cave canem* which means in Latin, "watch out for the dog." [3]Usually the dog the Romans were warning people about was the Italian greyhound, which the Ancient Romans kept as house pets. [4]The Italian greyhound of the time was somewhat less than 12 inches high and weighed between 6 and 10 pounds. Can you infer what the Ancient Romans were worried about with their *cave canem* signs?

Your conclusion: _____

Which sentences have the best evidence to support your conclusion? _____ _____

SPEAKING DUTCH

| pleasant | | nuts | pan | tall | homesick |
| island | fracture | | expensive | toothpaste | morning |

Write the English words from the choice box that match the Dutch words below.
Some Dutch words are spelled incorrectly to make them easier to pronounce.

1. breuk   _____

2. morgen   _____

3. kookpot   _____

4. tandpasta   _____

5. duur   _____

6. groot   _____

7. heimwee   _____

8. prettig   _____

9. eiland   _____

10. noten   _____

NOW THAT IS FAST

Read the true story below, then make an inference
based on the evidence in the story.

[1]Centuries ago, things moved far more slowly that they do today. [2]In the days before trains, airplanes, and automobiles, people could travel as fast as a horse could carry them on land and as fast as the wind could blow them in a sailing ship. [3]However, in the 1700s, one kind of boat was built to travel on a special kind of water that could reach speeds of 60 miles an hour while carrying six to eight passengers. [4]This kind of boat is still around today. Can you infer what kind of boat we are talking about?

Your conclusion: _____

Which sentence has the best evidence to support your conclusion? _____

SCRAMBLED U.S. STATES

Kyuckent	onOgre	kOahoaml	iganMchi
iaVingri	alMnadyr		nsKsaa
askNaerb	deNava		ssMriiou

Unscramble the words in the choice box to correctly spell
the name of a U.S. state that matches the clue below.

1. _____   Detroit's state

2. _____   the "Mother of Presidents"

3. _____   St. Louis' state

4. _____   Annapolis is the capital

5. _____   the Cornhusker State

6. _____   state famous for gambling

7. _____   Pacific Coast state, Salem is the capital

8. _____   the Bluegrass State

9. _____   the Sunflower State

10. _____   the Sooner State

TRY IT, YOU'LL LIKE IT

*Read the true story below, then make an inference
based on the evidence in the story.*

[1]We know that a word in one country can mean one thing and the same word-sound in another country can mean something quite different. [2]Back in 1928, one American company decided that the people of China would enjoy their product that was popular in America. [3]However, when the name of the product was pronounced in Chinese it translated to either "female horse fastened with wax" or "bite the wax tadpole." [4]Sales were poor until the company came up with the phonetic sound for its product of, "k'o k'ou k'ole," which translated into "permit the mouth to rejoice."   Can you infer the name of this American product?

Your conclusion: _____

Which sentence has the best evidence to support your conclusion?   _____

PRESIDENTIAL NAME GAME

Using the letters in the names of our twentieth president and his wife, write smaller words that match the definitions on each line below. The letters will always be in order either from left to right or right to left, and may be separated by other letters.

JAMES ABRAM & LUCRETIA GARFIELD

1. _____   antonym of false

2. _____   to frighten

3. _____   to boast

4. _____   weak or delicate

5. _____   a type of serious show

6. _____   agricultural business

7. _____   visions you have when you sleep

8. _____   a way of weaving long hair

9. _____   left, center, or right in baseball

10. _____   to attract, or artificial fish bait

DID IT ALL PAN OUT?

Read the story below, then make an inference based on the evidence in the story.

¹One of the more popular Greek gods in Greek mythology is the god Pan, the god of woods and pastures and the protector of shepherds and their flocks. ²In ancient Greece, there were lots of shepherds, which may explain his popularity. ³Pan was usually depicted as a creature who was half man and half goat. ⁴He had many love affairs and chased the nymph, Syrinx, who was changed into a bed of reeds. ⁵Making the best of a bad situation, Pan made a "panpipe" from the reeds and became famous for the beautiful music he played. ⁶Pan's main power was in his ability to fill men's minds with sudden, unreasoning terror. What modern word do we owe to Pan's strange power?

Your conclusion: _____

Which sentence has the best evidence to support your conclusion? _____

SPEAKING GREEK

radish	historical	office	score	pig
pelican	salmon	gray	lotion	news

Write the English words from the choice box that match the Greek words below. Some Greek words are spelled incorrectly to make them easier to pronounce.

1. skorara _____

2. solomos _____

3. rapani _____

4. nea _____

5. ghrafio _____

6. grizos _____

7. istorikos _____

8. losion _____

9. pelecanos _____

10. ghuruni _____

FAMILIAR SONGS?

*Read the true story below, then make an inference
based on the evidence in the story.*

[1]The following list of songs all have something in common. [2]They are, "Where the Columbines Grow," "Yankee Doodle," "Old Folks at Home," "Georgia on My Mind," "On the Banks of the Wabash, Far Away," "My Old Kentucky Home," "The Old North State," and "Oklahoma." Can you infer what all these songs have in common with each other?

Your conclusion: _____

Which sentence has the best evidence to support your conclusion? _____

SPEAKING PORTUGUESE

foreign	earth	wife	grateful	flat
father	farmer	writer	nurse	hat

*Write the English words from the choice box that match the Portuguese words below.
Some Portuguese words are spelled incorrectly to make them easier to pronounce.*

1. terra   _____

2. agricultor   _____

3. pai   _____

4. enfermeiro   _____

5. esposa   _____

6. escritor   _____

7. chapeu   _____

8. plano   _____

9. estrangeiro   _____

10. grato   _____

STATE OF THE UNION

Read the true story below, then make an inference based on the evidence in the story.

[1]Each of the fifty states in the United States is unique in comparison with each other, as they all have different names, different sizes, different populations, and so on. [2]Rhode Island's official name is, "State of Rhode Island and Providence Plantations." [3]This gives Rhode Island one of two size distinctions, each at opposite ends, that makes Rhode Island unique among all the 50 states. Can you infer Rhode Island's two size distinctions that sets it apart from the other 49 states?

Your conclusion: _____

Which sentences have the best evidence to support your conclusion? _____ _____

PRESIDENTIAL NAME GAME

Using the letters in the names of our twenty-first president and his wife, write smaller words that match the definitions on each line below. The letters will always be in order either from left to right or right to left, and may be separated by other letters.

CHESTER ALAN & ELLEN ARTHUR

1. _____   to be watchful

2. _____   antonym of early

3. _____   to be dishonest on a test

4. _____   our planet

5. _____   a rental agreement

6. _____   your physical condition

7. _____   older than 12 but younger than 20

8. _____   collapsible shelter used in camping

9. _____   begin

10. _____   body part above the waist, below neck

HAVE YOU NO COUTH?

*Read the true story below, then make an inference
based on the evidence in the story.*

¹The use of buttons, as we know them today, dates back to the 1200s in Europe. ²Before that time, people used various means to fasten their clothes, such as hooks or string. ³In the 1500s, rows of buttons on men's coat sleeves made their first appearance. This fashion continues to this day and men's suit jackets still have rows of buttons on the sleeves. ⁴These sleeve buttons seem to serve no purpose other than decoration, as the buttons are never used. ⁵But back in the 1500s, the buttons on the coat sleeves were put there to prevent men from engaging in a nasty habit. Can you infer what habit the buttons were trying to prevent?

Your conclusion: _____

Which sentence has the best evidence to support your conclusion? _____

SPEAKING TAGALOG

| sauce | yellow | statue | fresh | zucchini |
| purple | route | vacation | special | temple |

*Write the English words from the choice box that match the Tagalog words below.
Some Tagalog words are spelled incorrectly to make them easier to pronounce.*

1. dilaw _____

2. sukini _____

3. bakasyon _____

4. templo _____

5. monumento _____

6. espesyal _____

7. sawsawan _____

8. ruta _____

9. murado _____

10. presko _____

THAT'S NOT WHAT WE CALL IT!

Read the true story below, then make an inference
based on the evidence in the story.

[1]It often happens that the U. S. Navy will give a ship an official name and the sailors who sail on the ship will call it by another name. [2]For instance, the U.S. Navy deploys a ship called a destroyer and the sailors call it a "tin can," because of the way it bounces around in rough seas and because of its thin armor. [3]During World War II, the Navy built a ship designed to go right up to a beach, where most of the shooting was taking place, and land troops, weapons, and tanks right into battle. [4]The Navy called this ship an LST, which it said stood for "Landing Ship Tank." [5]It was fairly big, it wasn't very fast, and it went up close to where all the shooting was going on, so the LST sailors claimed the initials LST stood for something else. Can you infer what the sailors said the initials LST stood for?

Your conclusion: _____

Which sentence has the best evidence to support your conclusion? _____

FIGURE OUT THE ORDER

The five longest rivers in the world are, all in alphabetical order, the Amazon, the Chang, the Huang, the Nile, and the Ob. To determine their ordinal positions from first through fifth, use the clues below to cross out answer choices in the chart listing all the possibilities. When all the possibilities for each choice are crossed off except for one, the remaining answer must be correct.

FIRST	SECOND	THIRD	FOURTH	FIFTH
Amazon	Amazon	Amazon	Amazon	Amazon
Chang	Chang	Chang	Chang	Chang
Huang	Huang	Haung	Haung	Haung
Nile	Nile	Nile	Nile	Nile
Ob	Ob	Ob	Ob	Ob

1. Chang is longer than at least two other rivers, but it is not the longest river.

2. Huang is longer than the Ob, but Huang is shorter than the Chang.

3. The Amazon isn't the longest river, but it is longer than the Chang.

BREAK IT UP!

*Read the true story below, then make an inference
based on the evidence in the story.*

[1]The Roman Empire went into decline after 400 A.D. and became less able to protect itself from barbarian tribe invasions. [2]The tribe known as the Franks invaded and conquered the part of the Roman Empire that is today modern France. [3]Other tribes, such as the Huns, were more interested in loot than in territory and invaded and departed after getting what they wanted. [4]One tribe didn't seem to want either territory or loot, but seemed more interested in the malicious destruction of property than of anything else. [5]This tribe is famous for senseless destruction and its name is used today to describe anyone who destroys something. Can you infer the name of this tribe that is a modern word used to describe the needless destruction of property?

Your conclusion: _____

Which sentence has the best evidence to support your conclusion? _____

PRESIDENTIAL NAME GAME

*Using the letters in the names of our twenty-second and twenty-fourth
president and his wife, write smaller words that match the definitions
on each line below. The letters will always be in order either from left
to right or right to left, and may be separated by other letters.*

STEPHEN GROVER & FRANCES CLEVELAND

1. _____ color between blue and yellow or inexperienced

2. _____ free from harm or container for valuables

3. _____ a moaning sound

4. _____ a part in a movie or play

5. _____ to frighten

6. _____ to let fall or a tiny bit of rain

7. _____ a flat or even surface

8. _____ take what doesn't belong to you

9. _____ above or maybe finished

10. _____ jumping amphibian

STATE OF CONFUSION?

Read the true story below, then make an inference
based on the evidence in the story.

[1]Most state nicknames have a common-sense origin. [2]Nebraska is the "Cornhusker State" and you can deduce they grow a lot of corn in Nebraska. [3]But the state of Indiana is called the "Hoosier State" and nobody is quite sure how it got that name or even what a Hoosier really is. [4]Many scholars have decided that the name comes from an expression the early settlers of Indiana used when anyone came knocking on their doors. [5]Most people ask something like "Who is it?" if someone knocks on their door, but early Indianans said something different, which caused people to call them Hoosiers. Can you infer what the early Indianans asked when someone came knocking at their doors to give them the nickname of Hoosiers?

Your conclusion: _____

Which sentence has the best evidence to support your conclusion? _____

SPEAKING DUTCH

plum	mother	oyster	writer	backache
noodles	rain	quiet	port	napkin

Write the English words from the choice box that match the Dutch words below.
Some Dutch words are spelled incorrectly to make them easier to pronounce.

1. rugpijn   _____

2. moeder   _____

3. noedels   _____

4. servet   _____

5. haven   _____

6. oester   _____

7. pruim   _____

8. stil   _____

9. regen   _____

10. schrijver   _____

MAY I HAVE THIS DANCE?

*Read the true story below, then make an inference
based on the evidence in the story.*

[1]Before movies became really popular, theaters used to have live entertainment acts performing every day in something called vaudeville. [2]Vaudeville was simply a series of unrelated acts that could include singers, dancers, jugglers, comedians, and so on. [3]Many of the early stars of motion pictures, radio, and television first worked in vaudeville. [4]One dancer became extremely popular in the 1900s for his frantic trotting, and crazy dances that caused a sensation wherever he performed. [5]People seeing him dance wanted to imitate his steps and eventually a slower, less crazy, dance was created by ballroom dancers that still contained elements of the original dance. [6]Today, this dance is a commonly performed ballroom dance. [7]The original dancer's first name was Harry. Can you infer his last name and the dance that bears his last name?

Your conclusion: _____

Which sentence has the best evidence to support your conclusion? _____

FIGURE OUT THE ORDER

The five countries with the largest populations are, in alphabetical order, Brazil, China, India, Indonesia, and the USA. To determine their ordinal order from first through fifth, use the clues below to cross out answer choices in the chart listing all the possibilities. When all the possibilities for each choice are crossed off except for one, the remaining answer must be correct.

FIRST	SECOND	THIRD	FOURTH	FIFTH
Brazil	Brazil	Brazil	Brazil	Brazil
China	China	China	China	China
India	India	India	India	India
Indonesia	Indonesia	Indonesia	Indonesia	Indonesia
USA	USA	USA	USA	USA

1. Indonesia doesn't have the most people, but since it has more people than at least Brazil, Indonesia doesn't have the fewest people, either.

2. The USA has more people than Indonesia, but the USA doesn't have the most people, either.

3. India has fewer people than China, but it has more than the USA.

FOOD FOR THOUGHT

Read the true story below, then make an inference
based on the evidence in the story.

¹The basis of the ancient Roman diet of 2,000 years ago was fairly simple. ²The ancient Romans ate a lot of wheat, mostly in the form of bread, and a lot of olive oil. ³The ancient Romans did eat other vegetables, such as beans, lettuce, and peas; and fruits, such as grapes, apricots, cherries, and peaches; but mostly they ate bread. ⁴Finally, in the 1500s, the Romans started eating chocolate, corn, peanuts, peppers, pineapples, sweet potatoes, white potatoes, squash, and tomatoes. Can you infer the reason why the Romans waited so long before eating all those delicious and wonderful foods?

Your conclusion: _____

Which sentence has the best evidence to support your conclusion? _____

PRESIDENTIAL NAME GAME

Using the letters in the names of our twenty-third president and his wives, write smaller words that match the definitions on each line below. The letters will always be in order either from left to right or right to left, and may be separated by other letters.

BENJAMIN, CARRIE & MARY HARRISON

1. _____   a word by which we know you

2. _____   tunnel dug for minerals or ore

3. _____   edible plant seed found in pods

4. _____   large, animal that scared Goldilocks

5. _____   small fruit of blue, black, or straw

6. _____   a speed contest

7. _____   a protective crust over a sore

8. _____   feeling of regret for doing wrong

9. _____   not any at all

10. _____   an automobile

A SALUTE TO FLAGS

Read the true story below, then make an inference based on the evidence in the story.

[1]In case anyone asks, the study of the history and symbolism of flags is called "vexillology." Many national flags have interesting and logical origins. [2]For instance, the Danish King Valdemar the Victorious, saw a white cross appear in a red sky just before he won a battle in the 13th century. [3]Naturally, the Danish flag is now red with a white cross. [4]In 1191, Duke Leopold of Austria engaged in a particularly bloody battle during the Third Crusade. [5]After the battle, when Duke Leopold removed his blood-soaked clothes, he noticed his cloak was covered with blood except for where he wore his belt. Can you infer the country of Austria's flag design?

Your conclusion: _____

Which sentence has the best evidence to support your conclusion? _____

SPEAKING GREEK

waiter	oven	new	world	sweater
telephone	purse	sugar	November	priest

Write the English words from the choice box that match the Greek words below. Some Greek words are spelled incorrectly to make them easier to pronounce.

1. neos   _____

2. furnos   _____

3. Noemvrios   _____

4. papas   _____

5. portofoli   _____

6. zaketa   _____

7. zakhri   _____

8. tilefono   _____

9. garson   _____

10. kozmos   _____

OH, FUR GOODNESS SAKES!

*Read the true story below, then make an inference
based on the evidence in the story.*

¹Humans wearing fur-bearing animal skins dates back to prehistoric times. ²Prehistoric humans wore animal skins on their bodies for warmth and protection and used furs for bedding, rugs, and wall hangings around their shelters. ³Even after humans had learned to weave various materials into clothing, blankets, and rugs, there was still a strong demand for furs. ⁴Much of North America was explored by fur trappers looking for good trapping grounds. ⁵At one time or another, fur trapping was carried out in territory that now comprises 49 out of the 50 states. ⁶The only state where no fur trapping ever took place was in the state of Hawaii. Can you figure out why no animals were ever trapped for their fur in Hawaii?

Your conclusion: _____

Which sentence has the best evidence to support your conclusion? _____

FIGURE OUT THE ORDER

According to the United Nations, the five cities with the largest population in the world are, in alphabetical order, Bombay, Mexico City, New York, Sao Paulo, and Tokyo. To determine their ordinal positions from first through fifth, use the clues below to cross out answer choices in the chart that lists all the possibilities. When all the possibilities under each choice are crossed out except for one, the remaining answer must be correct.

FIRST	SECOND	THIRD	FOURTH	FIFTH
Bombay	Bombay	Bombay	Bombay	Bombay
Mexico City	Mexico City	Mexico City	Mexico City	Mexico City
New York	New York	New York	New York	New York
Sao Paulo	Sao Paulo	Sao Paulo	Sao Paulo	Sao Paulo
Tokyo	Tokyo	Tokyo	Tokyo	Tokyo

1. Mexico City is larger than three other cities, but it is not the largest.

2. New York is not the largest or the smallest, but it is larger than Bombay.

3. Sao Paulo is not as large as Mexico City, but Sao Paulo is not the smallest city, as it is larger than New York.

'WOOD' YOU STATE YOUR NAME?

Read the true story below, then make an inference
based on the evidence in the story.

¹Several U.S. states begin with "New," such as New Jersey, New York, and New Hampshire. ²We almost had a state "New Wales," named after the country of Wales, a part of Great Britain. ³The founder of the colony that was later to become a state proposed that name to King Charles II of England. ⁴However, a Welsh advisor to the king objected, so the king rejected "New Wales." ⁵The founder then thought about reports he had received concerning his land. ⁶One described his land as "sylvan," a fancy way of saying the land had a lot of trees. ⁷The founder then submitted a form of the word sylvan to the king, who added the founder's name to that word and a state eventually got its name. What is the name of this state?

Your conclusion: _____

Which sentences have the best evidence to support your conclusion? _____ _____

PRESIDENTIAL NAME GAME

Using the letters in the names of our twenty-fifth president and his wife, write smaller words that match the definitions on each line below. The letters will always be in order either from left to right or right to left, and may be separated by other letters.

WILLIAM & IDA MCKINLEY

1. _____ not bright, a weak bulb

2. _____ eat dinner

3. _____ unlocks a lock

4. _____ not tame

5. _____ murder perhaps

6. _____ U.S. state famous for lobsters

7. _____ where wheat is ground into flour

8. _____ part of a candle that burns

9. _____ a relative

10. _____ use the tongue to eat ice cream

IT'S NOT JUST PLAY

Read the true story below, then make an inference
based on the evidence in the story.

[1]The ancient Greeks of 700 B.C. had organized physical education programs for Greek boys. [2]These boys of 2,700 years ago received formal instruction in jumping, running, wrestling, and the throwing of the discus and the javelin. [3]Sometime later, the ancient Romans taught their boys many of the same activities, but emphasized those sports that had a military application. [4]After the fall of the Roman Empire in the 400s A.D., most physical education was in the military arts. [5]After about 1,000 years, the teaching of sports was revived and eventually resulted in the educational program we know today as physical education. Can you infer the name the ancient Greeks gave to their physical education facilities?

Your conclusion: _____

Which sentence has the best evidence to support your conclusion? _____

NATIONALITY RHYME TIME

amphibian	sin	freak	Greek	Swiss	deed	Welsh
French	belch	cotillion	Dutch	Italian	Libyan	bliss
Brazilian	Swede	drench	hutch	scallion	Finn	

Write two rhyming words from the choice box that match the clues below. The first
word in each set of clues has a geographic connection to the first answer word.

1. Greece weirdo   _____   _____

2. France soaking   _____   _____

3. Sweden action   _____   _____

4. Libya frog   _____   _____

5. Italy onion   _____   _____

6. Switzerland joy   _____   _____

7. Netherlands cabinet   _____   _____

8. Finland evil deed   _____   _____

9. Wales burp   _____   _____

10. Brazil dance   _____   _____

WAGONS WEST

*Read the true story below, then make an inference
based on the evidence in the story.*

¹In the 1840s, in the United States, settlers started crossing the Great Plains to reach destinations such as California and Oregon. ²They traveled in wagon trains and the main principle of such trains was to "keep moving." ³Wagon trains could only travel 15 to 20 miles a day and if the settlers hoped to cross the Rocky Mountains before snow blocked their way, they had to keep moving. ⁴These wagon trains had to cross territory belonging to the Plains Indians, who, during the 1840s and up to the late 1850s were often helpful. ⁵Some Indian tribes provided guides, some offered help at difficult river crossings, and some traded with the settlers, offering food for items carried by the settlers. ⁶All this changed in the late 1850s, when the pioneers started breaking a wagon train rule, which caused the Plains Indians to become hostile. Can you infer what these pioneers started to do in the late 1850s that angered the Plains Indians?

Your conclusion: _____

Which sentences have the best evidence to support your conclusion? _____ _____

SPEAKING PORTUGUESE

new	wind	man	learn	disappointed
power	column	peace	paper	leader

*Write the English words from the choice box that match the Portuguese words below.
Some Portuguese words are spelled incorrectly to make them easier to pronounce.*

1. desiludido _____

2. lider _____

3. aprender _____

4. homen _____

5. nova _____

6. papel _____

7. paz _____

8. poder _____

9. pilar _____

10. vento _____

THE PILGRIMS ARE COMING

Read the true story below, then make an inference
based on the evidence in the story.

[1]In 1620, 102 people set sail for America from England on the ship the Mayflower. During the voyage, one person died, but one was born, so 102 people made it across the Atlantic Ocean to land in what is now Massachusetts. [2]William Bradford, the second governor of the Plymouth Colony, founded by those Mayflower Pilgrims, wrote a history of the voyage. [3]Governor Bradford named most of the children who were on that first voyage. [4]He reported that there were 3 children named John, 2 named Joseph, and 2 named Mary. [5]The others were named William, Jasper, Love, Wresling, Richard, Ellen, Bartholomew, Remember, Priscila, Resolved, Perigriene, Giles, Constanta, Damaris, Oceanus, Francis, Henry, Humility, Eelizabeth, and Sammuell. Can you infer which of these children was the one born aboard the Mayflower when it was at sea?

Your conclusion: _____

Which sentence has the best evidence to support your conclusion? _____

PRESIDENTIAL NAME GAME

Using the letters in the names of our twenty-sixth president and his wives, write
smaller words that match the definitions on each line below. The letters will always be
in order either from left to right or right to left, and may be separated by other letters.

THEODORE, ALICE & EDITH ROOSEVELT

1. _____   to select or pick

2. _____   a perch for a bird or a chicken

3. _____   underground part of plant

4. _____   a bird of peace

5. _____   a smell

6. _____   to cast a ballot

7. _____   having life

8. _____   the back of the foot

9. _____   black substance formed by burning

10. _____   a popular flower

AN ARRESTING STORY

Read the true story below, then make an inference
based on the evidence in the story.

[1]Societies have long recognized the need for some kind of law enforcement officers. [2]In the 800s A.D. in England, a system was developed that was based on citizen responsibility. [3]The people were divided into groups of ten families and each group was responsible for the good conduct of its members. [4]Males, age 16 and older, were expected to take turns standing watch. [5]In the event of a serious crime, every adult male was expected to turn out to chase the criminal suspect. [6]Each county or "shire" in England had a leader or "reeve" whose responsibility was to supervise law enforcement in his area. [7]Today, in the United States, we still have a "shire reeve" as the chief law enforcement officer of a county. Can you infer the name of this law enforcement officer?

Your conclusion: _____

Which sentence has the best evidence to support your conclusion? _____

FIGURE OUT THE ORDER

The five largest inhabited continents in land area are, in alphabetical order, Africa,
Asia, Europe, North America, and South America. To determine their ordinal
positions from first through fifth, use the clues below to cross out answer choices
in the chart that lists all the possibilities. When all the possibilities under each
choice are crossed out except for one, the remaining answer must be correct.

FIRST	SECOND	THIRD	FOURTH	FIFTH
Africa	Africa	Africa	Africa	Africa
Asia	Asia	Asia	Asia	Asia
Europe	Europe	Europe	Europe	Europe
N. America	N. America	N. America	N. America	N. America
S. America	S. America	S. America	S. America	S. America

1. North America is larger than South America and Europe, but is smaller than two other continents.

2. Asia is larger than Africa and South America is larger than Europe.

THE 'MALE' MUST GO THROUGH

*Read the true story below, then make an inference
based on the evidence in the story.*

[1]Many ancient civilizations such as the Chinese, Egyptians, Persians, and Romans, developed well-organized mail systems. [2]These were necessary, as it enabled ancient rulers to communicate with all the areas of their empires. [3]The Greek historian Herodotus, in 400 B.C., wrote a description of the Persian mail system that is the motto of the U.S. Postal Service. [4]Herodotus wrote, "Neither snow, nor rain, nor gloom of night stays these couriers from the swift completion of their appointed rounds." [5]However, in none of the ancient civilizations mentioned did any of the great mass of citizens of these empires ever make use of these amazing postal systems. Can you infer the reason why the ordinary people in those times didn't send letters to anyone?

Your conclusion: _____

Which sentence has the best evidence to support your conclusion? _____

NATIONAL HOLIDAYS

Italy	England	Ireland	China	United States
Japan	France	Peru	Brazil	Mexico

Many countries share the same holidays, but some holidays are far more important in each of the countries listed in the choice box than they are in other countries.

Write the name of the country from the choice box that matches the holiday below.

1. Carnival   _____

2. St. Patrick's Day   _____

3. Buddha's Birthday   _____

4. Cinco de Mayo   _____

5. 4th of July   _____

6. Dragon Boat Festival   _____

7. Bastille Day   _____

8. St. Rose of Lima   _____

9. San Gennaro   _____

10. Boxing Day   _____

A GRAVE STORY

*Read the true story below, then make an inference
based on the evidence in the story.*

[1]When somebody dies and nobody is willing to pay for a proper funeral and burial, authorities have to dispose of the bodies. [2]This is a problem today and was a problem 2,000 years ago in Jerusalem. [3]One of the earliest-known references to such a burial ground is the story of Judas Iscariot, who was paid 30 pieces of silver to betray Jesus Christ. [4]Judas regretted his betrayal and gave the silver back to the priests. [5]The priests thought the money was tainted and decided to use it to buy land to be used as a free burial ground. [6]Fertile land was too expensive, so they arranged to buy land with poor clay soil unsuitable for farming and owned by a man who didn't mind the clay. Can you infer the occupation of the man who owned the land and what we call free, public burial grounds to this day?

Your conclusion: _____

Which sentence has the best evidence to support your conclusion? _____

PRESIDENTIAL NAME GAME

Using the letters in the names of our twenty-seventh president and his wife, write smaller words that match the definitions on each line below. The letters will always be in order either from left to right or right to left, and may be separated by other letters.

WILLIAM HOWARD & HELEN TAFT

1. _____ a flat, floating platform
2. _____ a tree often found weeping
3. _____ hand opposite of right
4. _____ water surrounding a castle
5. _____ person in charge of a prison
6. _____ part of a house you might paper
7. _____ tool to make holes or soldiers marching
8. _____ speak slowly like one from South
9. _____ one of Santa's helpers
10. _____ to give food to

FRANKLY PUZZLING

Read the true story below, then make an inference
based on the evidence in the story.

[1]Frank Thompson, one of the most famous soldiers of the American Civil War, enlisted in the Union Army in 1861, and served until the war ended in 1865. [2]Thompson became known as a master of disguise and was sent behind enemy lines as a spy. [3]Thompson completed one mission disguised as a black male laborer, another as a white female peddler, and still another disguised as a black female cook. [4]After the war, Thompson belonged to an organization of Union veterans called the "Grand Army of the Republic." [5]However, Frank Thompson was different from every other veteran in one respect which wasn't known until after the war. Can you infer what set Frank Thompson apart from many other civil war veterans?

Your conclusion: _____

Which sentence has the best evidence to support your conclusion? _____

FOREIGN PHRASES

in a large group	socially poised	method of operation	solid ground
the final blow	a lot of nerve	feeling of happening before	
have a good meal	unlucky person	temperamental person	

Many foreign phrases or words have come into common use in the United States. They have been taken from the Latin, French, Yiddish, Russian, Greek, Italian, and Spanish languages.

Write the English meanings from the choice box next to
the foreign word or phrase that matches below.

1. *modus operandi* _____

2. *coup de grace* _____

3. *bon appetit* _____

4. *déjà vu* _____

5. *chutzpah* _____

6. *en masse* _____

7. *schlemiel* _____

8. *savoir faire* _____

9. *terra firma* _____

10. *prima donna* _____

A WARRIOR PRINCE

Read the true story below, then make an inference
based on the evidence in the story.

[1]Edward is the name of one of the greatest warriors in English history. [2]Edward fought his battles in the 1300s, when warriors still wore armor. [3]Although Edward was never king himself, he was the eldest son of King Edward III, and the father of King Richard II. [4]Edward's first major battle was when he was only 16 and led a wing of his father's army against the French in the Battle of Crecy. [5]It was at this battle that he gained the name the "Black Prince," by which he is known throughout history. [6]Ten years later, the Black Prince commanded the English army that defeated the French in the Battle of Poitiers and captured the French king. [7]These are two of the most famous battles in English history. Can you infer the reason why they called Edward the Black Prince?

Your conclusion: _____

Which sentences have the best evidence to support your conclusion? _____ _____

FIGURE OUT THE ORDER

According to the Social Security Administration, the five most-popular boy
names in the 2000s are, in alphabetical order, Andrew, Jacob, Joshua,
Matthew, and Michael. To determine their ordinal positions from first
through fifth, use the clues below to cross out answer choices in the chart
that lists all the possibilities. When all the possibilities under each choice
are crossed out except for one, the remaining answer must be correct.

FIRST	SECOND	THIRD	FOURTH	FIFTH
Andrew	Andrew	Andrew	Andrew	Andrew
Jacob	Jacob	Jacob	Jacob	Jacob
Joshua	Joshua	Joshua	Joshua	Joshua
Matthew	Matthew	Matthew	Matthew	Matthew
Michael	Michael	Michael	Michael	Michael

1. Joshua, Matthew, and Michael were not either the most popular or the least popular of the top five most-popular names.

2. After Jacob, Michael was the most-popular name.

3. Matthew was not as popular a name as Joshua.

DANCING FEET

Read the true story below, then make an inference
based on the evidence in the story.

¹Magic is the supposed use of unnatural power by human beings. ²The belief in magical power has declined as scientific knowledge has increased. ³However, many people in more primitive societies still believe in magic, and even in modern societies, people consult fortune tellers and read their astrological charts. ⁴Some people engage in practices today without realizing they were once a form of magic. ⁵European folk dances, originally performed by peasant farmers, feature the dancers leaping as high into the air as possible. Can you infer what "magic" the original dancers from centuries ago were trying to cause to happen with their leaps?

Your conclusion: _____

Which sentence has the best evidence to support your conclusion? _____

PRESIDENTIAL NAME GAME

Using the letters in the names of our twenty-eighth president and his wives, write
smaller words that match the definitions on each line below. The letters will always be
in order either from left to right or right to left, and may be separated by other letters..

WOODROW, ELLEN & EDITH WILSON

1. _____   an unwanted plant

2. _____   toy with runners for sliding on snow

3. _____   hair from a sheep

4. _____   to slip or playground favorite

5. _____   revise your writing

6. _____   building material from a tree

7. _____   hole dug for water or oil

8. _____   rise and fall of the ocean

9. _____   person who works at a bank

10. _____   stay out of sight or an animal skin

A CATCHY TITLE

Read the true story below, then make an inference
based on the evidence in the story.

[1]Papyrus is a reedlike plant that grows along the Nile River in Egypt. [2]Ancient Egyptians discovered how to press papyrus into sheets of paper, which were usually pasted together to make rolls of paper of varying lengths. [3]Papyrus rolls were used throughout the ancient world but the only surviving rolls come from Egypt, because the dry climate of Egypt preserved them. [4]One common roll or book from ancient times is the one with prayers and hymns that was found in many tombs. [5]Modern translations of this Egyptian book are available today. [6]The ancient Egyptians didn't give a title to this book, so it was left to modern scholars to come up with a title. Can you infer by what logical name this ancient Egyptian book is known?

Your conclusion: _____

Which sentence has the best evidence to support your conclusion? _____

FOREIGN PHRASES

completely	that's life	a social blunder	full power
going on forever	unwelcome person	of unsound mind	
in place of a parent	group spirit	zest for life	

Many foreign phrases or words have come into common use in the United States. They have been taken from the Latin, French, Yiddish, Russian, Greek, Italian, and Spanish languages.

Write the English meanings from the choice box next
to the foreign phrase that matches below.

1. *joie de vivre*   _____

2. *faux pas*   _____

3. *esprit de corps*   _____

4. *carte blanche*   _____

5. *ad infinitum*   _____

6. *c'est la vie*   _____

7. *in loco parentis*   _____

8. *persona non grata*   _____

9. *non compos mentis*   _____

10. *in toto*   _____

ANYTHING TO HELP

Read the true story below, then make an inference
based on the evidence in the story.

[1]The Maya were an American Indian people who built an impressive civilization in Central America, which lasted from about 250 A.D. to about 850 A.D. [2]They were remarkable architects, painters, potters, sculptors, astronomers, and mathematicians. [3]The Maya were very religious and constructed huge pyramids for religious ceremonies and as burial chambers for kings and other important people. [4]They believed in an afterlife and buried their dead with personal items, tools, and utensils thought to be of use in the world to come after death. [5]If you were really rich and important, perfectly healthy people were killed and buried with you. Can you infer who these people were?

Your conclusion: _____

Which sentences have the best evidence to support your conclusion? _____ _____

FIGURE OUT THE ORDER

According to the Social Security Administration, the five most popular girl names in the 2000s are, in alphabetical order, Emily, Emma, Hannah, Madison, and Olivia. To determine their ordinal positions from first through fifth, use the clues below to cross out answer choices in the chart that lists all the possibilities. When all the possibilities under each choice are crossed out except for one, the remaining answer must be correct.

FIRST	SECOND	THIRD	FOURTH	FIFTH
Emily	Emily	Emily	Emily	Emily
Emma	Emma	Emma	Emma	Emma
Hannah	Hannah	Hannah	Hannah	Hannah
Madison	Madison	Madison	Madison	Madison
Olivia	Olivia	Olivia	Olivia	Olivia

1. Hannah wasn't as popular as Emma.

2. Emma wasn't as popular as Madison.

3. Madison wasn't as popular as Emily.

4. Olivia was less popular than Hannah.

A FISH STORY

*Read the true story below, then make an inference
based on the evidence in the story.*

[1]Early American Indians along the Atlantic Coast of North America used to take advantage of every resource available to them to get food. [2]The Indians hunted, fished, gathered wild foods, and engaged in agriculture to put food in their stomachs. [3]One fish was relatively easy to catch because it swam in huge schools near the surface. [4]But these fish are very bony and almost impossible to eat and, in fact, the Indians rarely ate them. [5]However, the Indians did make good use of these fish. [6]The Indian name for these fish is "Menhaden" and so they are called today. But can you infer what the English meaning of the word Menhaden is and what use the Indians made of the Menhaden?

Your conclusion: _____

Which sentences have the best evidence to support your conclusion? _____ _____

PRESIDENTIAL NAME GAME

Using the letters in the names of our twenty-ninth president and his wife, write smaller words that match the definitions on each line below. The letters will always be in order either from left to right or right to left, and may be separated by other letters.

WARREN GAMALIEL & FLORENCE HARDING

1. _____ small, brown song bird

2. _____ not right or correct

3. _____ name of a common wild duck

4. _____ fabric symbol of a country

5. _____ the glowing part of a fire

6. _____ pear-shaped fruit used in cookies

7. _____ farm that raises cattle

8. _____ not dirty

9. _____ wealthy

10. _____ tool to twist or tighten nut on a bolt

RUN FOR YOUR LIFE!

*Read the true story below, then make an inference
based on the evidence in the story.*

[1]In 490 B.C. the Greek city-state of Athens won a great victory against an invading Persian army. [2]The battle was fought on a plain located about 26 miles from Athens. [3]The name of this battle is remembered not because of the battle itself, but because of Pheidippides, a runner who didn't even fight in the battle. [4]When the Persians landed, the Athenians sent him running 150 miles to Sparta for help and then he ran back to tell them that Sparta wasn't coming right away. [5]The Athenians then attacked the Persians and soundly defeated them. [6]Pheidippides then ran 26 miles or so to Athens to tell of the victory. [7]He arrived and said, "Rejoice we conquer," and dropped dead. [8]Today, a type of race is run that is named after the battle that caused Pheidippides to run about so much. Can you infer the name of the battle and the race?

Your conclusion: _____

Which sentences have the best evidence to support your conclusion? _____ _____

FOREIGN PHRASES

an accomplished fact	what will be will be	compared with
newly wealthy	appropriate in fact	genuine
small group taking power	best of the best	reason for being

Many foreign phrases or words have come into common use in the United States. They have been taken from the Latin, French, Yiddish, Russian, Greek, Italian, and Spanish languages.

*Write the English meanings from the choice box next to
the foreign word or phrase that matches below.*

1. *apropos*   _____

2. *crème de la crème*   _____

3. *bona fide*   _____

4. *coup d'etat*   _____

5. *de facto*   _____

6. *fait accompli*   _____

7. *nouveau riche*   _____

8. *que sera sera*   _____

9. *raison d'etre*   _____

10. *vis-à-vis*   _____

A COLONIAL COIN

*Read the true story below, then make an inference
based on the evidence in the story.*

[1]Money can be anything that people agree to accept in exchange for items sold or work done. [2]A man might work for a farmer and receive a cow in payment. [3]However, a cow is hard to spend and people much prefer getting paid in coins that are easy to spend. [4]In the 1600s, there was a shortage of silver coins in the Massachusetts Bay Colony. [5]In 1652, the English government agreed to let the colony mint its own silver coins. [6]Massachusetts immediately began issuing a "Pine Tree Shilling," and, being silver, it was widely accepted as money. [7]However, the British government changed its mind and in that same year, forbade the minting of any additional coins. [8]Massachusetts pulled a trick on the British government and kept issuing the coins until 1682, before the British caught on. Can you infer what the Massachusetts colony did to fool the British?

Your conclusion: _____

Which sentences have the best evidence to support your conclusion? _____ _____

MATCH THE NATIONALITY

Hungarian	Indian	Irish	Spanish	Mexican
Turkish	Chinese	Swedish	Egyptian	Italian

Write the nationality from the choice box that matches the items below.

1. _____ hat dance, jumping bean

2. _____ towels, baths

3. _____ meatballs, furniture

4. _____ egg rolls, chopsticks

5. _____ paprika, goulash

6. _____ pyramids, mummies

7. _____ saris, Hinduism

8. _____ linens, crystal

9. _____ spaghetti, marble

10. _____ olives, bullfights

LUCKY LINDY

*Read the true story below, then make an inference
based on the evidence in the story.*

[1]One of the most famous people in the first half of the 20th century was Charles Lindbergh, who was the first person to fly solo across the Atlantic Ocean. [2]He flew across the Atlantic Ocean in 1927, in a single-engine plane named, "The Spirit of St. Louis." This is now on display at the Smithsonian Institution in Washington, D.C. [3]Other people had flown across the Atlantic Ocean before him, but Lindbergh was the first person to do it alone. [4]This feat caught the imagination of millions of people all around the world and Lindbergh was showered with awards, celebrations and parades wherever he went. [5]For a time, Lindbergh was the most famous person in the world. [6]In 1927, he wrote a book entitled *We* about his solo flight across the ocean. [7]But *We* is a pronoun that includes a group and Lindbergh was alone when he flew, so can you infer who Lindbergh was including when he titled his book *We*?

Your conclusion: _____

Which sentence has the best evidence to support your conclusion? _____

CITIES OF THE WORLD

Germany	Italy	France	Egypt	Ireland
Japan	South Korea	Russia	Canada	Spain

*Write the country from the choice box next to the two cities
that are located in this country. No capital cities are listed.*

1. Lyon   Marseilles   _____

2. Florence   Venice   _____

3. Montreal   Toronto   _____

4. Osaka   Kyoto   _____

5. Cork   Limerick   _____

6. St. Petersburg Novosibirsk   _____

7. Barcelona   Valencia   _____

8. Frankfurt   Cologne   _____

9. Pusan   Inchon   _____

10. Alexandria   Luxor   _____

ANSWERS

Note: The sentence evidence answers are based on the conclusions listed.

Page 1 The Wars of the Roses

Best evidence sentence(s): 3, 4

1. Paris, France
2. London, England
3. Moscow, Russia
4. Rome, Italy
5. Berlin, Germany

Page 2 A fifth leg

Best evidence sentence(s): 2, 4

1. Alaska		5. Iowa
2. Mexico		6. Canada
3. Erie		7. Atlanta
4. Rico		8. New York

Page 3 Winnipeg, the capital of the province of Manitoba

Best evidence sentence(s): 2, 3

1. WASH	6. SHIN
2. NOTE	7. MASH
3. SAW	8. WING
4. GEM	9. RAM
5. GRAIN	10. RASH

Page 4 Miners. Early Wisconsin lead miners dug caves in the sides of hills rather than build houses.

Best evidence sentence(s): 3 (The title also offers some evidence for this answer.)

1. Rome poem	6. French trench
2. Turk smirk	7. Pole mole
3. Spain drain	8. Scot plot
4. Egypt crypt	9. Brazil thrill
5. Greek peek	10. Swiss miss

Page 5   The Great Fire of London. The Great Fire of 1666 actually destroyed 87 churches.

Best evidence sentence(s): 1, 2 (The title also offers some evidence for this answer.)

1. Europe	6. baby food
2. dress	7. cut
3. depart	8. guide
4. cup	9. hospital
5. airplane	10. mail

Page 6   Any answer showing danger is correct. It is too dangerous for a horse and rider and only a sure-footed goat can travel safely on the trail.

Best evidence sentence(s): 4

1. Nepal   The only vowels in each word are "e and a".
2. Argentina   The words alternate beginning with "a" then "i".
3. Russia   The last letter of the first country is the first letter of the next one.

Page 7 Zipper

Best evidence sentence(s): 1, 3

1. SAD	6. MAD
2. HAM	7. JAM
3. NAIL	8. BAIL
4. BIG	9. JOB
5. HAIL	10. NAG

Page 8 A book.   Only people who could read would be interested in this product.

Best evidence sentence(s):   4

1. Tokyo, Japan
2. Beijing, China
3. Ottawa, Canada
4. Cairo, Egypt
5. Dublin, Ireland

Page 9 The wind shifted and blew the bombs back into the Austrian army.

Best evidence sentence(s): 4

1. Cuban Reuben	6. Finn din
2. Miami Grammy	7. Texas Lexus
3. Yankee hanky	8. Italian stallion
4. Brit mitt	9. Norway doorway
5. Dane pain	10. Swede deed

Page 10 Alberta. The province of Alberta.

Best evidence sentence(s):   1, 3

1. two	6. double
2. August	7. telephone
3. ferry	8. receipt
4. market	9. backpack
5. taxi	10. catalog

Page 11 "The Star Spangled Banner" uses the music, but not the lyrics to "To Anacreon in Heaven."

Best evidence sentence(s): 5

1. NEAT	6. SEAT
2. EAT	7. NOT
3. NOSE	8. SEAT
4. REST	9. NEST
5. TON	10. HERON

Page 12 They are paid to be the co-rulers of Andorra.

Best evidence sentence(s): 2

Congress	Truths
Oath	Utmost
New York	Trial
Speech	Interpret
The Bill of Rights	Official
Illegal	North Carolina

Page 13 Native Americans liked apples, too. Western Indians traded with Indians to the east for apple seeds and planted them around their villages.

Best evidence sentence(s):   2, 4

1. zero	6. backpack
2. Saturday	7. arrival
3. summer	8. sand
4. night	9. snow
5. boat	10. profit

Page 14 We celebrate April Fools Day in their memory.

Best evidence sentence(s): 7, 8

1. Monaco The first four words all have exactly 2 "os"
2. Estonia The words are in a, b, c order and end with a.
3. Andorra The first four words all have one set of double consonants.

Page 15 Atlantic Ocean

Best evidence sentence(s): 4

1. JOLLY	6. DEAD
2. MOON	7. SOLO
3. DAY	8. SILO
4. JELLY	9. MESS
5. MOLD	10. DOLL

Page 16 *Australis* is the Latin word for "southern," which explains how Australia got its name and the South African *"Australopithecus"* got a similar name.

Best evidence sentence(s): 2, 3

1. Rhine dine	6. Yellow bellow
2. Nile pile	7. Thames stems
3. Po snow	8. Seine train
4. Shannon cannon	9. Murray surrey
5. Oder motor	10. Rhone crone

Page 17 The animal is, of course, the goat. The term is "scapegoat."

Best evidence sentence(s): 2

1. father	6. candy
2. door	7. chicken
3. sailors	8. dictionary
4. accident	9. famous
5. boot	10. pastry

Page 18 The Tower of Babel. Meaningless sounds are called "babble."

Best evidence sentence(s): 6

Wife	Nation
Adams	General
Statesman	Tory
Hero	Orator
Independence	Notable

Page 19 "Barbe" is the French word for whiskers and "queue" is French for tail. They were having a good old-fashioned barbeque.

Best evidence sentence(s): 2

1. France trance
2. Libya tibia
3. Greece fleece
4. Venice tennis
5. Missouri flurry
6. Dutch touch
7. Wales sales
8. sand band
9. Peru guru
10. Chile billy

Page 20 Bears fight by swinging their arms down and bulls fight by hooking with their horns and swinging upward.

Best evidence sentence(s): 2, 3

1. ZOO
2. JAR
3. BET
4. TEASE
5. TAIL
6. MEAL
7. BONE
8. ROAM
9. LATE
10. MAZE

Page 21 The Beothuk painted themselves red. They became known as "red Indians" and soon all Indians were considered red.

Best evidence sentence(s): 3

1. Yangtze All the words have the "an" combination in the middle of the word.
2. Gambia All the words end with 2 different vowels.
3. Attu All the words begin and end with a vowel.

Page 22 Sir Benjamin was called "Big Ben." "Big Ben" is the bell in the clock tower of the Houses of Parliament and is a famous British landmark.

Best evidence sentence(s): 2, 4

1. airplane
2. soldier
3. travel
4. trust
5. bag
6. book
7. bus
8. court
9. easy
10. doctor

Page 23 Archery, because the bow and arrow were important weapons of war at the time.

Best evidence sentence(s): 3

Senate	Eight
Union	Case
President	Opinion
Ruling	Unjust
Elder	Reason
Majority	Tenure

Page 24 Justice of the Peace

Best evidence sentence(s): 3, 5

1. MADLY	6. CLOUD
2. JOIN	7. MAIL
3. YOU	8. SAY
4. DAY	9. CLAM
5. SIN	10. LOUD

Page 25 Jack, and the holiday decoration is the Jack O' Lantern.

Best evidence sentence(s): 4

1. airplane	6. market
2. baby	7. meat
3. laundry	8. nurse
4. jacket	9. pajamas
5. kitchen	10. pineapple

Page 26 Lucy Hayes refused to allow any alcoholic beverages of any kind in the White House.

Best evidence sentence(s): 4

1. Congo bongo	6. Malay delay
2. Czech deck	7. Berlin twin
3. Ohio bayou	8. Maine brain
4. Indonesia anesthesia	9. Serb curb
5. Manila vanilla	10. Idaho crow

Page 27 The expression is "highball" as in "let's highball it out of here."

Best evidence sentence(s): 6

1. library	6. toothpaste
2. mother	7. waiter
3. parent	8. sunglasses
4. raincoat	9. cough
5. school	10. button

Page 28 Ice. New England had plenty of ice in the winter and it was a welcome product in locations where ice was scarce.

Best evidence sentence(s): 4

Cars	Organic
Agriculture	Raisin
Los Angeles	National
Iceberg	Interstate
Fajitas	Avocado

Page 29 Telephone directories list each person's occupation in addition to names and addresses.

Best evidence sentence(s): 6

1. RACK	6. REASON
2. SALE	7. NEW
3. REACH	8. REEL
4. DEW	9. ARK
5. LEAD	10. WRECK

Page 30 Meteorites is the best guess. This is where prehistoric people probably got their hands on iron.

Best evidence sentence(s): 6

1. guide	6. ashtray
2. conference	7. orange
3. United States	8. walnut
4. Ping-Pong	9. cherry
5. ballet	10. money

Page 31 According to the Constitution, the minimum age of a senator is 30 years old. When Henry Clay was appointed at age 29, no one challenged him so he was allowed to serve.

Best evidence sentence(s): 2, 3

1. schilling drilling	6. rupee loopy
2. krone stone	7. yen pen
3. franc rank	8. pound round
4. real heal	9. guilder builder
5. mark dark	10. dollar holler

Page 32   The goats stayed up all night.

Best evidence sentence(s): 4, 5

1. dictionary	6. inside
2. father	7. mouse
3. field	8. padlock
4. government	9. pottery
5. hike	10. selfish

Page 33   A "big wig" describes a self-important person.

Best evidence sentence(s): 3

1. MAN	6. RAT
2. TAR	7. NEAR
3. MARE	8. TAN
4. TIN	9. VAN
5. RUN	10. RUB

Page 34   Constable

Best evidence sentence(s): 5

1. ocean	6. suitcase
2. drugstore	7. toothpaste
3. radio	8. waitress
4. serious	9. yogurt
5. spider	10. allergy

Page 35   Crater Lake had no fish until trout were introduced to the lake in 1888.

Best evidence sentence(s): 4

Lisbon	Taipei
Athens	Universal
Tokyo	Denver
Istanbul	Edinburgh

Page 36   It was called a mule. A mule is a cross between a "jenny" and a horse, so calling it a mule makes some kind of sense.

Best evidence sentence(s): 3 (The title also offers some evidence for this answer.)

1. factory   6. home
2. fast   7. heat
3. great   8. kill
4. influenza   9. lake
5. jam   10. love

Page 37 President Taft threw out the first pitch to start the baseball season.

Best evidence sentence(s): 3

1. YELL   6. HARE
2. SHARE   7. WAR
3. RAY   8. HEN
4. WILL   9. HILL
5. LEAN   10. RARE

Page 38 Tasman sailed completely around Australia without sighting it. Tasman did see it
        2 years later on another voyage.

Best evidence sentence(s): 5

1. sculpture   6. surprise
2. tomato   7. drinking straw
3. waiter   8. shampoo
4. zoo   9. police
5. switch   10. potato

Page 39 The tarantula spider did the biting.

Best evidence sentence(s): 3

1. Canada   6. Australia
2. Egypt   7. Greece
3. Spain   8. Russia
4. China   9. Germany
5. Switzerland   10. Ireland

Page 40 Nadezhda insisted they never meet in person and only communicate by letters.

Best evidence sentence(s): 7

1. two   6. style
2. sunrise   7. polo
3. express   8. restaurant
4. driver   9. snack
5. toilet   10. soup

Page 41 Batteries, of course. The knowledge of how to make batteries dates long before
any power plants were ever built.

Best evidence sentence(s): 5

1.	LATE	6.	LIAR
2.	HEAR	7.	TILE
3.	LATTE	8.	NET
4.	LETTER	9.	REAL
5.	HEAT	10.	JOY

Page 42 The Romans paved their roads.

Best evidence sentence(s): 5, 6

1.	mouth	6.	flashlight
2.	antiseptic	7.	hat
3.	clock	8.	police
4.	airplane	9.	reservation
5.	circus	10.	short

Page 43 Choking. All previous harnesses went around a horse's neck causing it to choke
if the load was too heavy. Horses could pull 5 times as much in one load.

Best evidence sentence(s): 3

1.	Superior	6.	Indian
2.	Mexico	7.	Bering
3.	Atlantic	8.	English
4.	Michigan	9.	Pacific
5.	Victoria	10.	Dead

Page 44 The tumbleweeds were scattering seeds which grew into weeds that had to be
pulled by the farmers in the spring and summer.

Best evidence sentence(s): 4

1.	sugar	6.	ancient
2.	sunny	7.	borrow
3.	tiny	8.	cantaloupe
4.	weather	9.	child
5.	burn	10.	mother

Page 45 They were marking the depth of the river. The term "mark twain" is two fathoms
or about 12 feet.

Best evidence sentence(s): 4

1.	PRANK	6.	LOOK
2.	RAP	7.	OAK
3.	POEM	8.	LARK
4.	MARK	9.	PARK
5.	POSE	10.	HARM

Page 46 Osiris was the Egyptian god of crops or vegetation of most importance to farmers.

Best evidence sentence(s): 4

1.	bad	6.	perfume
2.	cookie	7.	rice
3.	baseball	8.	sandal
4.	castle	9.	scalp
5.	number	10.	soup

Page 47 The Dead Sea

Best evidence sentence(s): 5

1.	mountain fountain	6.	navy's gravies
2.	ocean notion	7.	sea's bees
3.	equator debater	8.	chart tart
4.	king bling	9.	soccer locker
5.	river's shivers	10.	Sphinx drinks

Page 48 Death's Head Moth

Best evidence sentence(s): 4

1.	market	6.	permission
2.	matches	7.	room
3.	necklace	8.	rope
4.	oven	9.	singer
5.	past	10.	shampoo

Page 49 Washington created the award. Washington called it the "Badge of Military Merit" and it was given for bravery. Since1932, the Purple Heart has been awarded solely for wounds and death.

Best evidence sentence(s): 5

1.	CHART	6.	MAYOR
2.	MARRY	7.	HALO
3.	OATH	8.	ROT
4.	CARRY	9.	GRAY (OR GREY)
5.	TEAR	10.	YEAR

Page 50 Denim

Best evidence sentence(s): 4

1. patient	6. goose
2. newspaper	7. gnat
3. luggage	8. fruit
4. library	9. drapes
5. intersection	10. desert

Page 51 Dido cut the hide into extremely thin strips and laid them out to outline a large area.

Best evidence sentence(s): 5

1. Mountain	6. Caesar
2. Washington	7. Belgium
3. Pole	8. Liberty
4. Gettysburg	9. New York
5. Light	10. Memorial

Page 52 Dollar

Best evidence sentence(s): 1, 4

1. CALL	6. MILLION
2. FILM	7. LIME
3. ALARM	8. CAROL
4. ROOM	9. FAIL
5. LABOR	10. DIAL

Page 53 The punishment for almost every crime, no matter how minor, was death.

Best evidence sentence(s): 4

1. dessert	6. bakery
2. apple	7. bicycle
3. doctor	8. coffee
4. airline	9. engine
5. luggage	10. ice cream

Page 54 Underwriting. Risk takers wrote their names "under" the ship and cargo that were being insured.

Best evidence sentence(s): 6, 7

Venison	Indians
Initial	North Carolina
Richmond	Irate
George	Atlantic

Page 55 Uranium

Best evidence sentence(s): 5

1. PIECE	6. RICE
2. PIER	7. RAIN
3. FRANCE	8. LIP
4. PAIN	9. RIPE
5. CRANK	10. ANKLE

Page 56 Ravens were thought to know where the nearest land was. If lost, the Vikings would release a raven and sail in the direction it flew to find land.

Best evidence sentence(s): 4, 5

1. ambulance	6. highway
2. center	7. enter
3. tour	8. liver
4. new	9. papaya
5. plate	10. blackberry

Page 57 Virginia

Best evidence sentence(s): 3

1. White	6. Bull
2. Columbus	7. English
3. Rose	8. Tower
4. King	9. Stone
5. David	10. Hill

Page 58 Volcanoes

Best evidence sentence(s): 6

1. nose	6. wallet
2. peanut	7. wash
3. puncture	8. hammock
4. salt	9. intermission
5. towel	10. mud

Page 59 In 1850, soda water began being bottled. When opened it, made that "pop" sound causing people to start calling it "soda pop."

Best evidence sentence(s): 4

1. MULE	6. BANANA
2. CHANNEL	7. HUB
3. BARREL	8. TEAM
4. MEET	9. BURN
5. NICE	10. CANE

Page 60 Spain

Best evidence sentence(s): 5

Very!	Frostbite
Army	Ordeal
Leader	Revolutionary
Launch	George
Encampment	Endure
Yield	

Page 61 Man, who crawls on all fours as a baby, then walks on two legs, and finally, in old age, requires a cane to walk.

Best evidence sentence(s): 6

1. stairway	6. shampoo
2. tea	7. science
3. tomato	8. night
4. watch	9. map
5. wind	10. library

Page 62 The Statue of Liberty Frederic Auguste Bartholdi was the sculptor of the Statue of Liberty and modeled the face after his mother.

Best evidence sentence(s): 4, 5

1. LOOM	6. BARN
2. BRAT	7. LAMB
3. TOOL	8. ARM
4. ODD	9. MALL
5. HARD	10. TOLL

Page 63 Steeplechasing The men agreed to "race to yon steeple."

Best evidence sentence(s): 5

1. Rock
2. General
3. Court
4. table
5. pie
6. tip
7. flakes
8. plates
9. home
10. Cape

Page 64 To allow the sun and moon to pass by, of course.

Best evidence sentence(s): 6

1. shape
2. speed
3. throat
4. sun
5. voice
6. wash
7. tweezers
8. yellow
9. tooth
10. king

Page 65 Bandages

Best evidence sentence(s): 2

1. haze
2. jaw
3. noon
4. lion
5. reason
6. seed
7. drew
8. soil
9. soar
10. wed

Page 66 Ferris. George W. Ferris

Best evidence sentence(s): 3

1. cookie
2. crime
3. cake
4. book
5. bathroom
6. address
7. bandage
8. soap
9. hat
10. tea

Page 67 The number is 21. Each number after the first two numbers equals the sum of the two numbers that come before it.

Best evidence sentence(s): 4

1. Helsinki	6. Beirut
2. Bombay	7. Wellington
3. Havana	8. Warsaw
4. Shanghai	9. Lisbon
5. Budapest	10. Ankara

Page 68 The "scarlet scourge" was lipstick from wives and girlfriends kissing the V-mail before mailing it.

Best evidence sentence(s): 7, 8

1. SPY	6. SESSION
2. MISS	7. SIP
3. PANT	8. RINSE
4. RAISE	9. LIAR
5. YES	10. LESS

Page 69 "Hello." Edison said he got the idea from the word, "Halloo," used in fox hunting to call the hounds to the chase.

Best evidence sentence(s): 4

1. classical	6. wool
2. heart	7. contest
3. hat	8. diary
4. long	9. walking trail
5. tin can	10. traffic

Page 70 A quarter is still commonly referred to as "two bits."

Best evidence sentence(s): 3

1. warm	6. hockey
2. Spain	7. corner
3. thermometer	8. shuttle
4. office	9. eight
5. fingernail	10. wool

Page 71 "Graveyard of the Atlantic"

Best evidence sentence(s): 4

1. FORD	6. RICH
2. ORCHARD	7. HAY
3. HIRE	8. BIRCH
4. YARD	9. RULE
5. THIRD	10. BUY

Page 72 The Romans were trying to protect their dogs from being stepped on.

Best evidence sentence(s): 2, 4

1. fracture	6. tall
2. morning	7 homesick
3. pan	8. pleasant
4. toothpaste	9. island
5. expensive	10. nuts

Page 73 Iceboats on frozen lakes and rivers.   In the 1700s, Dutch settlers in the Hudson River area of New York built wind-blown iceboats that traveled faster than anything else in that era.

Best evidence sentence(s): 3

1. Michigan	6. Nevada
2. Virginia	7. Oregon
3. Missouri	8. Kentucky
4. Maryland	9. Kansas
5. Nebraska	10. Oklahoma

Page 74 Coca-Cola

Best evidence sentence(s): 4

1. TRUE	6. FARM
2. SCARE	7. DREAM
3. BRAG	8. BRAID
4. FRAIL	9. FIELD
5. DRAMA	10. LURE

Page 75 Panic or pandemonium

Best evidence sentence(s): 6

1. score	6. gray
2. salmon	7. historical
3. radish	8. lotion
4. news	9. pelican
5. office	10. pig

Page 76 These are all official states songs. In order, they are Colorado, Connecticut, Florida, Georgia, Indiana, Kentucky, North Carolina, and Oklahoma.

Best evidence sentence(s): 2

1. earth
2. farmer
3. father
4. nurse
5. wife

6. writer
7. hat
8. flat
9. foreign
10. grateful

Page 77 Rhode Island has the longest official state name and is the smallest state in area.

Best evidence sentence(s): 2, 3

1. ALERT
2. LATF
3. CHEAT
4. EARTH
5. LEASE

6. HEALTH
7. TEEN
8. TENT
9. START
10. CHEST

Page 78 Men would wipe their noses and their mouths with their sleeves. (Some still do.)

Best evidence sentence(s): 5

1. yellow
2. zucchini
3. vacation
4. temple
5. statue

6. special
7. sauce
8. route
9. purple
10. fresh

Page 79 Large Slow Target

Best evidence sentence(s): 5

FIRST	SECOND	THIRD	FOURTH	FIFTH
Nile	Amazon	Chang	Huang	Ob

EXPLANATION. Cross off Chang under FIRST, FOURTH, and FIFTH as it isn't the longest and is longer than at least two other rivers. For clue 2, cross off Huang and Ob under FIRST and SECOND as they are shorter than Chang. For clue 3, cross off Amazon under FIRST meaning Nile must be FIRST as the only remaining possibility and you may cross out Nile under all the other choices. Clue 3 says Amazon is longer than Chang and Chang had to be SECOND or THIRD so Amazon must be SECOND and Chang must be THIRD. Cross out Amazon and Chang under the other answer choices. Clue 2 says Huang is longer than Ob so Huang must be FOURTH and Ob must be FIFTH. Puzzle is solved.

Page 80 Vandal or Vandals, or vandalize

Best evidence sentence(s): 5

1. GREEN	6. DROP
2. SAFE	7. LEVEL
3. GROAN	8. STEAL
4. ROLE	9. OVER
5. SCARE	10. FROG

Page 81 They said, "Who's here?" or "Who is here?"

Best evidence sentence(s): 5

1. backache	6. oyster
2. mother	7. plum
3. noodles	8. quiet
4. napkin	9. rain
5. port	10. writer

Page 82 Harry Fox gave his name to the foxtrot.

Best evidence sentence(s): 4

FIRST	SECOND	THIRD	FOURTH	FIFTH
China	India	USA	Indonesia	Brazil

EXPLANATION. Clue 1 allows you to cross off Indonesia under FIRST and under FIFTH as it doesn't have the most and it has more than Brazil so it can't be FIFTH either. Clue 1 also allows you to cross out Brazil under FIRST and SECOND as it has fewer than Indonesia and we know Indonesia isn't FIRST so Brazil can't be SECOND as it comes after Indonesia. Clue 2 tells you to cross off USA under FIRST, FOURTH, and FIFTH as it doesn't have the most people but it has more than both Indonesia and Brazil. Clue 3 tells you to cross off India under FIRST leaving China as the only choice left under FIRST. Clue 3 also tells you to cross off India under THIRD, FOURTH, and FIFTH as it is larger than the USA which is larger than both Indonesia and Brazil. India must be SECOND. USA must be THIRD as it is larger than Indonesia and Brazil. Indonesia is larger than Brazil so it must be FOURTH and Brazil must be FIFTH. Puzzle is solved.

Page 83 All were foods not known until after Columbus discovered America in 1492.

Best evidence sentence(s): 4

1. NAME	6. RACE
2. MINE	7. SCAB
3. BEAN	8. SHAME
4. BEAR	9. NONE
5. BERRY	10. CAR

Page 84 Red with a white stripe

Best evidence sentence(s): 5

1. new
2. oven
3. November
4. priest
5. purse

6. sweater
7. sugar
8. telephone
9. waiter
10. world

Page 85 Hawaii has no fur-bearing animal to trap.

Best evidence sentence(s): 6 (The title also offers some evidence for this answer.)

FIRST	SECOND	THIRD	FOURTH	FIFTH
Tokyo	Mexico City	Sao Paulo	New York	Bombay

EXPLANATION. Clue 1 tells you Mexico must be SECOND as it is larger than 3 other cities but not in FIRST place. Clue 2 allows you to cross out New York under FIRST and FIFTH and to cross out Bombay under FIRST, SECOND, and THIRD because it is smaller than New York and New York can't be FIRST or SECOND. Clue 3 allows you to cross off Sao Paulo under FIRST meaning Tokyo is the FIRST, and Sao Paulo under FIFTH meaning Bombay must be the answer under FIFTH. The only remaining possibility for Sao Paulo must be THIRD as it is larger than New York and New York is larger than Bombay so it must be FOURTH. Problem is solved.

Page 86 Pennsylvania was founded by William Penn.

Best evidence sentence(s): 6, 7

1. DIM
2. DINE
3. KEY
4. WILD
5. KILL

6. MAINE
7. MILL
8. WICK
9. KIN
10. LICK

Page 87 Gymnasiums

Best evidence sentence(s): 5

1. Greek freak
2. French drench
3. Swede deed
4. Libyan amphibian
5. Italian scallion

6. Swiss bliss
7. Dutch hutch
8. Finn sin
9. Welsh belch
10. Brazilian cotillion

Page 88 The pioneers didn't always "keep moving" and started to settle in the Great Plains.

Best evidence sentence(s): 2, 6

1. disappointed	6. paper
2. leader	7. peace
3. learn	8. power
4. man	9. column
5. new	10. wind

Page 89 Oceanus, of course.

Best evidence sentence(s): 5

1. CHOOSE	6. VOTE
2. ROOST	7. ALIVE
3. ROOT	8. HEEL
4. DOVE	9. SOOT
5. ODOR	10. ROSE

Page 90 Sheriff is derived from "shire reeve."

Best evidence sentence(s): 6

FIRST	SECOND	THIRD	FOURTH	FIFTH
Asia	Africa	N. America	S. America	Europe

EXPLANATION. Clue 1 means North America must be THIRD and Europe and South America can't be FIRST, SECOND, and THIRD, and Asia and Africa can't be THIRD, FOURTH, or FIFTH. Do all the crossing-out and Clue 2 tells you that Asia must be FIRST, Africa must be SECOND, South America must be FOURTH, and Europe must be FIFTH. Problem B is solved.

Page 91 Only a tiny percentage of the people could read or write.

Best evidence sentence(s): 5

1. Brazil	6. China
2. Ireland	7. France
3. Japan	8. Peru
4. Mexico	9. Italy
5. United States	10. England

Page 92 He was a potter. Free burial grounds have been called "potter's fields" ever since.

Best evidence sentence(s): 6

1. RAFT
2. WILLOW
3. LEFT
4. MOAT
5. WARDEN
6. WALL
7. DRILL
8. DRAWL
9. ELF
10. FEED

Page 93 Frank Thompson was really Sarah Emma Evelyn Edmonds, a female who disguised herself as a male to join the army. (She was helped by a friend who formed the unit she joined.) She was the only female allowed into the G.A.R. after she wrote a book about her experiences.

Best evidence sentence(s): 3

1. method of operation
2. the final blow
3. have a good meal
4. feeling of happening before
5. a lot of nerve
6. in a large group
7. unlucky person
8. socially poised
9. solid ground
10. temperamental person

Page 94 Edward wore black armor at the Battle of Crecy.

Best evidence sentence(s): 2, 5

FIRST	SECOND	THIRD	FOURTH	FIFTH
Jacob	Michael	Joshua	Matthew	Andrew

EXPLANATION. Clue 1 allows you to cross out Joshua, Michael, and Matthew under FIRST and FIFTH and Andrew and Jacob under SECOND, THIRD, and FOURTH. Clue 2 tells you that Jacob is FIRST and Michael is SECOND. Clue 3 tells you that Joshua is THIRD, Matthew is FOURTH, and Andrew must be FIFTH.

Page 95 Scholars believe the high jumps were made to encourage the crops to grow tall,

Best evidence sentence(s): 5

1. WEED
2. SLED
3. WOOL
4. SLIDE
5. EDIT
6. WOOD
7. WELL
8. TIDE
9. TELLER
10. HIDE

Page 96 The Book of the Dead

Best evidence sentence(s): 4

1. zest for life
2. a social blunder
3. group spirit
4. full power
5. going on forever
6. that's life
7. in place of a parent
8. unwelcome person
9. of unsound mind
10. completely

Page 97 Servants Really important people needed servants in the next world.

Best evidence sentence(s): 4, 5

FIRST	SECOND	THIRD	FOURTH	FIFTH
Emily	Madison	Emma	Hannah	Olivia

EXPLANATION. Clue 1 tell you to cross out Hannah under FIRST and Emma under FIFTH. Clue 2 tells you to cross-out Emma under FIRST and Madison under FIFTH. Clue 3 tell you to cross out Madison under FIRST and Emily under FIFTH. Clue 4 tells you to cross out Olivia under FIRST and Hannah under FIFTH. If you did the crossing out you know that Emily is FIRST and Olivia is FIFTH. You should cross out Emily and Olivia under SECOND, THIRD, and FOURTH as we know their places. Now go back to clue 1 and Hannah is not as popular as Emma so Hannah is crossed out under SECOND and Emma is crossed out under FOURTH. Clue 2 tells you Emma was less popular than Madison so Emma is crossed out under SECOND. This leaves Madison as the only answer under SECOND and Emma the only answer under THIRD and Hannah as the only possible answer for FOURTH. Problem is solved.

Page 98 Fertilizer or "that which enriches the soil." Indian farmers used the Menhaden as fertilizer for their crops.

Best evidence sentence(s): 2, 5

1. WREN
2. WRONG
3. MALLARD
4. FLAG
5. FLAME
6. FIG
7. RANCH
8. CLEAN
9. RICH
10. WRENCH

Page 99 Marathon

Best evidence sentence(s): 2, 6

1. appropriate
2. best of the best
3. genuine
4. small group taking power
5. in fact
6. an accomplished fact
7. newly wealthy
8. what will be will be
9. reason for being
10. compared with

Page 100 Massachusetts issued all coins until 1682 with the date 1652.

Best evidence sentence(s): 7, 8

1. Mexican
2. Turkish
3. Swedish
4. Chinese
5. Hungarian
6. Egyptian
7. Indian
8. Irish
9. Italian
10. Spanish

Page 101 Lindbergh was referring to himself and his plane as the *We*.

Best evidence sentence(s): 6, 7

1. France
2. Italy
3. Canada
4. Japan
5. Ireland
6. Russia
7. Spain
8. Germany
9. South Korea
10. Egypt

FREE SAMPLE
from our award-winning
Mind Benders® A2 book.

10. Cars and Colors

The cars of Arnett, Bradley, Church, and Dawson are gray, red, silver, and yellow.

Find each person's name and car color.

1. Bradley and Church had lunch yesterday with the owner of the silver car.

2. Dawson saw the owners of the red car and the gray car passing his house yesterday.

3. The owner of the yellow car thinks he got a better deal on his car than Arnett and Dawson got on theirs.

4. Bradley's car is not a bright color.

Chart for Problem 10

	gray	red	silver	yellow
Arnett				
Bradley				
Church				
Dawson				